FOR AGES, herbs have served man as food, medicine, spiritual comforters and, supposedly, as exorcisers of demons, witches and other malign forces. Among these modest, unassuming bits of vegetation we find no blatant, noisome colors crying for attention. Of all the plants we grow in the garden, these are the most intimate, the most personal.

The true herbalist must know plants, appreciate their special virtues and live, eat and talk herbs on every possible occasion. Only a person who has lived on these familiar terms with herbs can possibly write about them with authority. I know of no one who qualifies more highly than the author of this volume.

Let me warn the casual reader against skipping idly through these pages, lest he be trapped unawares and find himself knee-deep in the fragrant mysteries of herbs.

—*R. Milton Carleton*
Herb Society of America

A Book of Herbs

Also by the author:

The Fairy's Garden
My Garden Gate Is on the Latch

A
Book of
Herbs

*How to grow herbs and
use them for seasoning, fragrance,
decoration and as natural cures
for common ailments*

By EDITH FOSTER FARWELL

Revised Edition

The White Pine Press
Piermont, New York

Revised edition, 1979

26th printing

Published by the White Pine Press, Inc.
Box 402, Piermont, New York   10968

This book was originally published under the title, "Have Fun With Herbs."

Special contributors to this edition: Bonnie Fisher, Peterstown, W. Va.; Seymour B. House, Bend, Ore.; Hollis Keats, Piermont, N.Y.; Daniel Schwartz, Boston, Mass.; Francis Sheild, Hampton, Va.

Cover design by Elaine Groh

Printed in the United States of America by the Bookmark Press, North Bergen, New Jersey. Set in English Times

Library of Congress Cataloging in Publication Data
Farwell, Edith Foster.
    A book of herbs.
"Originally published under the title, 'Have fun with herbs.' "
1. Herbs. 2. Herb gardening. 3. Cookery (Herbs).
4. Herbs—Therapeutic use. I. Title.
SB351.H5F37   1979   635'.7   79-22580

ISBN 0-935720-01-4

To the Chicago Horticultural Society

ACKNOWLEDGMENTS AND THANKS TO: *The Herb Grower* magazine for permission to use recipes of Isabella Gaylord, which previously appeared in their issues; the *Chicago Tribune*; Mrs. Elizabeth Mackey, for her herbs and recipe for "Quickies"; Benedikt Diethelm, friend and fellow gardener; Mrs. Margaret Dunsire; Mr. and Mrs. Edward Lehtinen, family companions who spent hours in our kitchen and garden trying out recipes and developing new gardening ideas; and to my husband Albert, who gave continual patience and advice.

—*E.F.F.*
Lake Forest, Ill.

Contents

Preface

THE HISTORY OF HERBS is really a history of mankind; the more you read about them, the more fascinated you're apt to become. You'll discover that an old herb garden is beautiful and lovable. The humble little plants ask for so little, and give so much.

An herb is a plant that is useful for medication, seasoning, fragrance, cosmetics or dyes. There are about 500 herbs commonly used today. To be able to grow even a handful of them, cut them when fresh and use them for seasoning, medicinal purposes and otherwise, is an experience everyone should have.

To work in a garden means much more than to grow just what a garden produces. Gardening is a way of life. It brings us close to the soil and gives us faith — faith that some great power will make that seed grow and burst into bloom.

E.F.F.

Foreword:
Getting started with herbs

By M.C. Goldman, executive editor,
Organic Gardening magazine

NEVER GROWN HERBS? You'll be surprised how simple it is to start a kitchen patch of these flavorsome little plants.

For centuries, gardeners and cooks in England, many other countries across Europe — and later in Colonial America — kept a patch or border of various herbs just outside the kitchen door. Herbs thrived there and stood ready, within easy reach for seasoning as meals were being prepared, or as foods were put up to store for wintertime tables.

Nostalgia aside, those old-time kitchen gardens make a lot of sense today. For one thing, you can't beat the aroma, flavor and enjoyment of your own fresh or dried herbs. And growing your own sure does beat the escalating costs of spices and seasonings on market shelves. Growing herbs is one more sensible step, albeit a modest one, towards self-sufficiency.

Getting an herb patch started is really one of the simplest of all gardening achievements. In fact, medieval books and backyarders called these plants "simples" because they grew so easily and provided basic remedies for many ailments of people and animals. Now all this folklore is being rediscovered, and there's a surge of new interest in old plants. The reason? New evidence that plants have remarkable healing powers. Researchers are now burrowing deep into ancient writings and coming up with surprisingly effective remedies for everything from bellyache and skin irritations to virus infections and kidney disease. Those with a special eye for certain weeds, herbs or trees are prowling mountainsides in the Orient, jungles in South America and coastlines in northern Europe to unearth raw materials for testing other primitive treatments. Drug firms are diverting attention from rapid-fire development of synthetic prescriptions to look diligently into more corners of botanical medication.

The revolution in plant healing has meant an about-face for a large segment of medical science, which for years scoffed at such natural remedies as backwoods superstition or outright witchcraft. Today's headlines have led previously cynical scientists to reexamine their prejudices. And well they might. Even the search for control of cancer has lately dealt with plants, and foremost among plants with age-old reputations for healing are the herbs. Some 400 or more have been given detailed recipes for preparation and recommended for a long list of ailments. "Herbals," as the old books devoted to medicinal herb use are still called, have been more heeded than almanacs or seed catalogues. Hieroglyphs from Mesopotamia and Egypt tell us of uses of anise, coriander and cumin by those practicing medicine more than 5,000 years ago, before the printed word.

Shepherds in early tribal communities observed the effects various plants had on animals. Applying their observations to humans, they became the medicine men of their tribes. From that time to the present, when scientists are now confident that the medical potential of plant life has not been fully explored, there is hope that continuing studies of nature's garden will produce new aids to mankind.

Choose several of the popular culinary herbs that serve a double purpose as healing aids. That way you'll have your own backyard botanical garden — herbs for seasoning and for trying medicinally. You'll find that quite a few home-garden herbs work well as insect pest deterrents, too.

So whether for seasoning or healing, decorating or fragrance, make this season the one you get started growing herbs!

1
American herbalists

MARION WILBUR lives for her garden. With such denizens as bloodroot (*sanguinaria canadensis*), jo-jo-ba (*simmondsia chinesis*) and shoofly (*nicandra physlodes*), it is no ordinary garden; but then, she is no ordinary gardener. Born in Poland, she moved to the U.S. at age three and has since lived in Pennsylvania, California and now Oregon. Five years ago her family moved from southern California to the sweeping hills that mark the terminus of the Oregon Cascades. Their herb farm, Casa Yerba, is 25 miles south of Roseburg on a valley side surrounded by pine and hardwoods. An Interstate highway is a dozen miles to the west, invisible.

"We moved here because we needed more land and lower taxes," Marion explains, gesturing with a sweep of her well-tanned arm towards the hills that rise immediately behind their house. "In southern California, the sky was brown, the air wasn't good." The Wilburs owned a cabin in the mountains outside Orange County which they visited on weekends. Now they live full time in that weekend environment with their animals and plants, and their lives have blossomed.

Marion Wilbur: A master with herbs, a close kinship to nature.

Photography courtesy of Organic Gardening magazine

"It takes a lot of work to live here," Marion says, indicating with a faint smile that it is well worth the effort. "When we first came to Casa Yerba the soil was mostly clay and rock. To dig you needed an auger, not a shovel." But hard work seems to have paid off; around the house are banks of flowering herbs that scent the air with myriad fragrances. And there is plenty of room to expand.

As she moves among the bees and blossoms, Marion is at home. In addition to hundreds of square feet of herbs, Casa Yerba also boasts two greenhouses (one indoors and one outdoors) that contain tropical plants and herbs such as maté and loquat, a building for drying seeds and leaves, and an open-air shed for sun-sensitive young herbs. For the Wilburs, herbs are a way of life. From the initial stages of cultivation and soil preparation to the glass of soothing tea or the healing poultice, growing herbs is the focus around which their days are centered. Work never ends, and it is only the rare week late in the fall when the family can travel. Not that they relish the chance to leave; life on the herb farm is its own form of relaxation, with all the necessary elements to a healthy and well-ordered lifestyle.

"We live with our herbs, so we stay pretty healthy," she says as she snaps a leaf from a lemon basil and crushes it between her fingers and passes it beneath her nose, sniffing approvingly. "I don't know where I picked up my interest in herbs — everywhere, I guess. My mother used herbs, and there are lots of good books about them. I just found out by myself."

Judging by such plants as a peculiar grapevine bursting from a wooden trellis, a variety that "isn't supposed to grow here," her success has been considerable. For Marion, herbs are the key to good health. "Most herbs have a medicinal quality," she explains, "and the herbs in an area are the best ones for an ailment you get there. For example, manzanita leaves around here can be used to treat poison oak."

To one less familiar with medicinal herbs, and that includes most everyone except the Wilburs, the benefits of herbal remedies may seem a bit quaint. But Marion has plenty of first-hand accounts of their potency. Herbal medicine is her prime interest and she is well-known for her remedies. Her family doctor has occasionally issued prescriptions, only to see her cure the ailment with herb treatments. "Many modern drugs are like insecticides," she says. "They kill off the friendly as well as the unfriendly — they don't discriminate."

At Casa Yerba, no insecticides are used. What is good policy for the garden is good policy for the body, she believes, and both seem to be thriving. Even the animals at the farm are sometimes given herbal teas to help recuperation or to prevent illness. "I'm not anti-medicine or anti-doctors," she says, "but I do like to use my own medicine when I find out what's in doctors' prescriptions. This is our greatest use for herbs. I call it our first-aid kit.

"Generally we are healthy, although I do see a doctor once a year. I don't think there is anything more rewarding in gardening than growing herbs. We live with them, and we never seem to get sick."

Stooping to pluck a weed from between two toothache plants (which, when crushed, ease the pain of an inflamed gum or aching tooth), Marion chuckles briefly. Holding the offending plant aloft she defines a weed: If you think it's there by accident, it's a weed; if not, it's an herb. "I guess it all depends on how familiar you are with the plant," she explains.

Among the basils and the mints at Casa Yerba are several easily recognizable weeds — all of them by design. Marion cultivates nettles, thistles, Queen Anne's Lace and several types of mullein, each for a particular reason. For her, a plant is a weed until she can figure out how to use it. She feels that many less dedicated gardeners limit themselves needlessly because of their lack of knowledge or, as is more often the case, by their lack of time. Marion spends the better part of every day in her garden, tending her plants and harvesting their benefits. When she isn't working the soil or transplanting new herbs, building a new greenhouse or concocting herbal teas and remedies, she may be found in her studio sculpting, or weaving pine-needle mats and straw baskets. The painstaking detail of her work indicates a closer kinship with nature than one is accustomed to. It bespeaks a person who is a master of plants in all their uses.

—S.B.H.

Cyrus Hyde

New Jersey is not noted for lush green gardens and pastoral hilltop vistas, despite the "Garden State" billing its auto license plates proclaim. It is an industry-riddled, densely populated chunk of land sandwiched between the industrial swathways of New York City and Philadelphia. Its saving graces, as far as an outdoor-minded person is concerned, are its long miles of Atlantic Ocean coastline and its less populated western edge. The latter, thankfully, holds a few incongruous, green-studded patches of rolling farmland.

Cyrus Hyde, a stocky, even-tempered Baptist with a reassuring smile, lives in one of these pockets. His home is Well-Sweep Farm, a four-and-one-half acre piece of land that is a haven for everything from show poultry and sheep to tarragon and table vegetables. This relatively small property produces virtually every item that appears on the family table. And along with these eatables there are herbs — more than 500 of them, as listed in Well-Sweep's last inventory. While the Hyde family — Cyrus and wife Louise and several children — live on the food they grow, they make their living from the farm's mail-order, herb-nursery and dried-flower business. Several hundred visitors find this hilltop mini-farm each week during the peak of the summer growing season, and during the winter they order plants and seeds by mail. Louise Hyde is "assistant foreman," and keeps the business books. She is also a culinary artist with herbs.

For all of Cyrus' liking for gardening and farming the organic way, a visitor can quickly see that herbs are his first love. He sees them as the most intriguing of all of nature's wild and nursery-cultivated growing things, and he has manifested his fascination in them by gathering herb species from all over the world. In his formal garden there are hundreds of exotic breeds, perhaps more varieties than any other one place in the U.S. In the lavender section, for example, there are about three dozen sweet-smelling varieties to boggle minds of visitors. Looking them over while giving a tour, Cyrus confesses, "Yes, I am a collector."

For the Hydes, the mini-farm is a six-day-a-week business, and everyone participates. On Sundays the family attends

Cyrus Hyde, of Well-Sweep Farm: "All my life is right here."
Photos by Hollis Keats

church, to which they give 10 percent of their annual earnings. This is Cyrus' way of recycling the spiritual rewards the land has given him. For recreation, he is Spartan. He seldom indulges in travel or suburban-style luxuries, so close, at hand in nearby Hackettstown (five miles away). He is fascinated by what his patch of land can produce, and all his energies are focused there. "I don't drink, smoke or play golf," he says. "All of my life is right here."

Cyrus grew up on a family homestead outside Paterson, New Jersey, back in the not-so-long-ago past when that New York City suburb was partial farm country. He liked rural life and worked as a dairyman, later as a milkman and then as a landscaper. In this last job he began experimenting with herbs, becoming an expert in his spare time. Later he became herbalist for the Waterloo Village Restoration in Stanhope. When time allowed, he and Louise began restoring a run-down farmhouse in Point Murray. This was Well-Sweep, into which they moved in the mid 1960's. At first it was no more than a series of thickets that entwined a house long since gone by. Today it is a well-kept yellow farmhouse-and-outbuilding layout, surrounded by organically enriched, productive land. The remainder tells its own story. At this writing the Hydes have been at Well-Sweep for 13 years.

—H.K.

Bonnie Fisher

Bonnie Fisher lives on a remote, 112-acre farm in Peterstown, West Virginia. She's understandably reluctant to tell anyone of the farm's whereabouts, since she and her husband Dave have seen as many visitors and as much of the urban-style life as they care to. They bailed out of city life — in this case, Akron, Ohio, in 1972 — looked for rural hideaways, and moved east for cherished peace and quiet. By all counts, their quest was successful. Their new home is one of the most isolated out-of-the-way farmlets east of the Mississippi, and it is the basis for a fulfilling, self-sufficient life.

Before her migration east, Bonnie was a schoolteacher; now she is an herb and vegetable farmer, gardening writer, and small businessperson (managing Hickory Hollow Farm, her own mail-order herb business). She is an expert in virtually every aspect of herbs, and writes frequently for *Organic Gardening* and *The New York Times*, in addition to other publications. Her latest herb cookbook is being issued by Keats Publishing Co. in New Canaan, Connecticut.

Nutrition is an area where Bonnie has particularly helped pioneer the use of herbs, as evidenced by her chapter, "Herbs as substitutes for salt" later in this book. "Your food has natural salt in it," she is quick to point out, "so there's no need to add more." The proven link between Americans' overzealous salt intake and high blood pressure and heart ailments has finally caused much thought about restricting diet habits. Bonnie has been instrumental as a writer and gardener in urging this redirection. (She also wrote "The fragrant herbs" chapter in this edition, and contributed numerous recipes.)

If she ever finds time to pull herself away from growing herbs, cooking with them, drying them for uses as fragrances, and using them in every imaginable way to provide a healthier life, Bonnie will undoubtedly have several more books forthcoming. In all likelihood, they will be must reading.

—H.K.

Opposite—Bonnie Fisher: "Your food has natural salt, so there's no need to add more." Herbs are good substitutes, she notes in Chapter 10.

Chuck and Toni Attmore

Tucked away about 20 miles north of Albuquerque, New Mexico, is the small farm of Chuck and Toni Attmore. They've been here since 1972, when Chuck ended a 30-year career term in the military. They started out growing herbs in addition to table vegetables for their own taste. "It was a subsistence farm," recalls Chuck, "and we had a lot of casualties." One problem was shade, which they eventually solved by shielding the plants from the New Mexico sun with artificial covers.

They began their herb garden with a shotgun approach: basils, fennels and mints, mostly. At first there were about 30 varieties of mints, and then, after two seasons, they narrowed down the selection. "After that," he says, "everything snowballed. People started finding us." The Attmores began selling herbs commercially, and business was good. Everything is hand-grown and hand-picked, and they have developed a considerable following. That kind of quality, notes Chuck, is the keynote to getting the most from herbs. Says he of more modern ways: "It's difficult to maintain quality with machines. If you harvest with them, the result quickly turns to hay." —D.S.

The Attmores: Making herbs flourish in the Southwest

Heinz Grotzke

Heinz Grotzke came to the U.S. from Germany in 1955, and has worked Meadowbrook, his 11-acre farm in Wyoming, Rhode Island, since 1966. He grows a wide variety of vegetables here, although they are for family use only. Most of his time is spent cultivating herbs and developing better ways to enrich and farm the earth. He is executive director of the Bio-Dynamic Farming and Gardening Association, edits "Bio-Dynamics" (the newsletter of that organization), and is recognized as one of the key authorities on herb cultivation in this country. Says he, a bit modestly, "All I do is put the seed in. Then I go away and see what happens."

That, in truth, oversimplifies the horticultural abilities of the man. A frequent visitor to Meadowbrook more aptly evaluates Heinz by appraising his land. Says she: "It's a place where you can *feel* the life of the whole organism."

Grotzke is active in affairs of the Bio-Dynamic Farming and Gardening Association, and is philosophical about the growing cycle of plants and the gardener's role in preparing good soil. Says he:

"On our type of garden, all different forms of life are seen in concentration. The planet earth is an organism, a living thing, and all functions are interrelated. You make use of the earth while you are alive, and you have to give something back. Composting symbolizes giving life back to the earth.

"A plant is a two-fold being, a being that follows two forces — one that leads it toward the earth, and another towards the sun. Physics pull the roots down; the sun pulls plants up. This is a manifestation of spirit — one part lives in darkness, one part lives in light.

"The basic needs for growing are air, warmth and water. If they are not in harmony, the whole process goes wrong. The gardener's job is to bring the three into harmony."

—H.K.

2

Growing

HERBS ARE PROBABLY the easiest of all plants to grow. They are not bothered by insects, and they will stand drought. Some will survive zero-degree temperatures, and many can be taken inside as house plants.

They should be grown in full sunlight and in well-drained soil. The earth should be friable — that is, able to be crumbled into small pieces when held in the hand. Little or no fertilizer is needed, as that has a tendency to make the plants large and luxuriant in appearance, but lacking in the oils that are necessary for the flavoring and fragrance of the leaves.

Only one or two of each variety is needed in order to provide sufficient flavoring for a family of four. Fresh herbs are always the best to use, although dried ones are very satisfactory.

To dry herbs, cut in July just before the plants come into flower; tie in bunches and hang in a dark, dry, airy place. At the end of two or three weeks, crumble each bunch so that the particles will fit through a sieve; then bottle for use.

Plant your culinary herb garden as near the kitchen door as possible, so as to have your plants handy to take a snip of this or that for flavoring. If you do not have space for a garden, try growing them in pots or boxes. All the plants mentioned in the plan on page 29 are easy to grow. Just remember that herbs need sun and a well-drained location.

If your garden plot is not a border layout (one you can walk around from the inside), but has paths all around it, place the high plants — lovage, French sorrel, etc. — in the center, and plant the lower herbs, as shown in the plan, around them. (To grow tarragon, you will have to buy plants, as it does not set seed.) If you are beginning an herb garden, I suggest you buy all the perennial plants. The annuals — chervil, sweet basil, and summer savory — come up readily from seed.

Location and soil

Most herbs need full sunlight to develop their essential oils. It is these oils that give flavor and fragrance to the plants.

Regular garden soil, evenly tilled and aired, is a satisfactory medium, but care must be taken to ensure that the soil is not too lean or sandy. Many gardeners prefer to use sterile potting soil, consisting of a mixture of vermiculite and peat moss. This has the advantage of being sterile and easy to handle. Germinating plants indoors and moving them outside when the summer is in full swing is quite popular, as it allows you to monitor the early stages of germination and to protect the plants from a killing frost. With annuals, frost tolerance is especially low, and transplanting should not be done until every possible danger of frost has passed.

If you plan to start herbs indoors, there are a few essential props that ensure proper conditions for the seeds to germinate. This equipment is the same for all herbs, annuals and perennials alike. First, fill a flat or tray with soil or with two-inch pots (the organic cardboard type work well). Suspend grow lights over these trays (Gro-Lux or any standard grow lights can be used) to within three inches of the soil. The lights should be arranged so that they can easily be raised to accommodate the growing plants. Two lights should be used over each flat: a warm white and a cool white.

After the seed is sown or planted and the soil is thoroughly moistened, a transparent covering is helpful in order to retain soil moisture (plastic wrap or glass is commonly used), but remember the seeds that require darkness in which to germinate (newspaper over the glass works well). The lights should be left on for 14 to 18 hours per day, and the soil should always be checked to make sure it does not dry out. Every few days the cover should be removed briefly to air out the flat and to water the soil. The herbs that require darkness to germinate are fennel (*Foeniculum vulgare*), lavender (*Lavendula augustifolia*), sage (*Salvia off*) and coriander (*Coriandrum sativum*).

Some seeds require planting as opposed to sowing. These should be planted roughly at a depth equal to their diameter. They are caraway (*Carum carvi*), chives (*Allium schoenprasum*), sage and parsley. All other seeds can be sown on the surface of the soil for proper germination. Germination time varies with each plant and sometimes with each seed batch, but generally those seeds planted indoors beneath grow lights will germinate faster than the same seeds outdoors. Certain seeds, such as parsley, take much longer to germinate than others, and you should not lose faith if it seems your parsley has failed to sprout. In addition, parsley seeds should be soaked for 24 hours in water (warm to the touch) prior to planting. Thyme is the only other seed that requires special preparation before planting; it must be frozen and thawed three times to ensure germination. Many of these indoor-growing tips are suggested by Marion Wilbur of Days Creek, Oregon.

Transplanting the indoor-germinated seedlings should not begin until all frost danger is past, and the first real leaves of the plant are seen. If your climate is hot and sunny, new plants should be allowed to "sun harden" before being permanently transferred outdoors. This process consists of placing the flats in the sun for a few hours a day and gradually increasing their tolerance to direct sunlight, much like conditioning your body against sunburn early in the summer. Plants germinated outside do not need this special treatment.

Once the seedlings are sun-hardened they are ready to be transplanted. The choice of location should be a sunny, accessible place with good soil. Pick a site that has full sun and good drainage. A spot of ground where water stands after a rain is not suitable for a garden until proper drainage has been made. For that, I would advise calling in an expert.

The area should be spaded deeply. With your foot on the spade, dig down the full length of it, turn the sod upside down and break it into fine pieces with the spade. If the earth seems sticky, add sand and dried leaves. Again, the earth for growing herbs must be friable — that is, able to be crumbled into small pieces when squeezed in the hand. After it is well broken-up, rake the earth smoothly, and you are ready to put in your seed. Caution: Any soil enrichment (by adding ordinary loam, for example) will cause an excess of foliage and the resulting minimum of flavor in leaves and seeds. Also, N.B.: Never burn your leaves. Keep them in a compost pile with other organic matter (i.e., lettuce leaves, tops of vegetables, weeds, melon, grapefruit or orange rinds — but no meats or fats). A little earth scattered over each layer, and in a year's time or so you'll have good black soil.

After the soil is prepared and moistened, indoor seedlings can be carefully transplanted (biodegradable pots are quite handy here) and watered, to avoid drying out. If you have an adequately long growing season, outdoor germination is usually best, as it requires no special measures. This way, seeds can be sown or planted in good garden soil.

Sowing seed

Be careful how you sow your seed. Plant to a depth of at least twice the diameter of the seed. Pour some of the seed from the packet into your left hand, and with your right hand take little pinches of the seed between your fingers and scatter them thinly along a row, or over the area where you want your plants. (If you're a southpaw, reverse the process.) Then press down firmly with the palm of your hand or the back of the hoe. If the seeds are large, scatter a bit of earth over them before you press them. If the soil is very dry, sprinkle it lightly from a watering can. Many people find it helpful to cover the seeds with a burlap bag during watering. This prevents them from washing away, and conserves moisture.

Care must be taken to avoid covering those seeds that germinate in light for too long, or poor germination may result. If the sun seems likely to scorch the sprouted plants, a few hours of shade during the hottest part of the day may prevent excessive water loss. This protective measure is necessary only in very hot climates when the seeds are just sprouting.

When three or four tiny leaves appear, thin out the bunches so they stand six to 10 inches apart. Do not start your annual seeds outdoors until danger of frost is past. When in doubt, consult your local garden shop or nursery for suggested planting schedules.

There are several common herbs that cannot, for one reason or another, be started from seeds and therefore must be grown from a cutting. In addition to these plants, there are some that are more easily begun by using available existing plants. For instance, chives are easily purchased in planters from many supermarkets, and when transplanted outdoors will thrive quite naturally. The same is true for garlic bulbs, though these should be planted in the fall. Any member of the mint (*Mentha*) family will grow easily when started from a bottom leaf placed in water until root hairs appear, and then transplanted to soil. And it is well-known how invasive mint can be; it requires occasional cutting back to prevent it from taking over some of the less aggressive herbs. Other exceptions are: French tarragon (*Artemisia dracunculus satavia*), which is sterile and cannot be started from seed. Rosemary (*Rosemarinus off.*) can be seed-started but is slow to germinate. It is best begun by taking a cutting. Lavender seeds must be fresh to ensure proper germination, as seed batches that are old usually fail to mature into a satisfactory crop.

As a general rule, the perennial herbs are much hardier than the annuals, and most kitchen herbs are perennial. Remember also that growing seasons vary from climate to climate, and that some seeds, as mentioned earlier, need a lot of coaxing.

But whatever the effort involved, a good herb garden is a delight. When the herbs are blooming and bees are darting about between the clumps of fragrant leaves, all the effort is rewarded.

Design of the herb garden

Every garden should have a definite design of some kind. It has been said that a garden should look as well in the winter as it does in the summer, the theory being that if there is a good design, the garden will always look well with or without plant-

For Border Planting of Culinary Herbs

A = ANNUALS
P = PERENNIALS

12 feet

5 feet

Garlic Chives • Parsley • Chives

French Sorrel (P)
Tarragon (P)

Lorage (P)
Tarragon (P)

French Sorrel (P)
Tarragon (P)

Summer Savory (A)

Sweet Basil (A)
Sage (P)

Summer Savory (A)

Sweet Marjoram

Chervil

Sweet Marjoram

Silver Thyme (P)

Kitchen Thyme (A)

Thyme (P)

Garlic Chives • Parsley • Chives

ing. A wall, fence, or hedge for a background makes a good beginning. The design on the first title page was taken from the Blair Kitchen Herb Garden in Williamsburg, Virginia. The diamond is set in a square, encircled by paths. It is an interesting study of a well-drawn design. No matter where you stand in this little garden, the lines are always good.

This diamond design can be applied to any size garden, using the diamond in the right proportion to the size of the bed. Read Sir Frank Crisp's book, "Mediæval Gardens," for designs of old gardens. Your public library may have it. I found it in the modest library in my home town.

Draw some designs for yourself during the winter months. Then, when you have drawn your own motif in the earth later in the season, you'll see your garden come to life.

I have created small dish gardens of herbs in designs that are lovely. To do this, fill a low dish with sand, moisten it, and place cuttings of teucrium, santolina, box and evergreens, just to name a few, in a design. The cuttings will root and the little dish garden will keep fresh for many weeks indoors. Later, these rooted cuttings can be potted up to make new plants.

If you do not have space for an herb garden, but do have a vegetable garden, tuck in a few plants of sweet basil next to your tomatoes, summer savory near the string beans, and garlic chives and parsley along your lettuce rows. (N.B.: These herbs should be in a place where they will not be disturbed by spring planting.)

3

Four herbs for the beginner

F OR THOSE JUST starting out, I suggest trying the
following four herbs. Learn how to grow and use them,
and perhaps find out something about their history.

Sweet basil (*ocimum basilicum*)

This is an annual that grows about three feet high. In India the
basil plant is sacred to both Krishna and Vishnu. The strong
aromatic scent in its leaves is much like that of cloves. It is said
that all Hindus go to rest with a basil leaf on their breasts,
reputedly as a passport to paradise.

Basil is also much used and honored by Italians, who claim it
"engenders sympathy between those who wear it." To
Moldavians, it is considered an enchanted flower of such
potency "that a man who accepts a sprig from a woman will love
her forever."

In Tudor days, small pots of basil were often given to visitors
by farmers' wives as pleasing compliments. Parkinson, the old
herbalist said, "The ordinary basil is in a manner wholly spent
to make sweet or washing waters among other sweet herbs, yet
sometimes it is put into nosegays. The physical properties are to

procure a cheerful and merry heart whereunto the seed is chiefly used in powder.''

Plant your basil seed out-of-doors in your garden as soon as danger of frost is over. It will germinate in five to 10 days. Cut the leaves all summer for use in flavoring any tomato or fish dish. If you want to cut it to dry, to use in the winter, I would advise planting the larger-type basil. Cut this in midsummer, tie it in bunches and hang in a dry, airy place. When the leaves are dry enough to crumble, put them through a strainer and place in a mason jar with top firmly on.

Bush Basil (*ocimum minimum*)

This interesting little plant is a low, bushy one that grows to about six inches in height. For the small garden or border, I prefer this basil. The flavor is like larger basil, but this plant is hardier. (Note that you can dig it up in the fall and pot it for use as a house plant.)

Chervil (*anthriscus cerefolium*)

"Sweet Chervil or 'Sweet Cis' is so like in taste unto Anise seeds that it much delighteth the taste among other herbs in a sallet."

—John Parkinson, Paradisus, 1629.

This herb was used by the Romans, so we know it is one of the oldest inhabitants of the garden. We also read of it in the 15th Century list of recipes as being one of the necessary plants for use in the kitchen. It is used extensively by the French, especially in their omelette with "fines herbes."

Another old herbalist wrote that chervil should "never be wanting in sallets as long as they may be had, being exceedingly wholesome and cheering the spirits."

Chervil is an annual that grows about eight inches high. Sow it in a well-drained soil as soon as danger of frost is over. The leaves are ready to be cut and used as soon as they are a few inches high. Make two or three sowings during the season to keep it continually growing. Use in salads, soups and stews. For seasoning, remember: one teaspoon of the fresh, cut in fine pieces, or one-quarter teaspoon of the dried herb serves four.

Sweet marjoram (*origanum marjorana*)

The botanical name, origanum, means "Joy of the Mountain," and one can not imagine a more appropriate name for this plant. We have sweet marjoram in our Shakespeare garden, with a quotation beside it from "All's Well That Ends Well": "Indeed, Sir, she was the sweet marjoram of the salad, or rather the herb of grace."

In ancient Greece it was believed that if marjoram grew on a tomb the person buried there was happy. Marjoram was one of the strewing herbs. It can be put in sweet bags for linen, in a "tussie-mussie" to enhance the fragrance of that little bouquet, and it can also be used for flavoring.

Marjoram seed takes a long time to germinate, so I would suggest buying a few plants or starting it in a pot in a sunny window during early spring. It is a perennial but not hardy in northern climates, so bring it indoors where it will make a most delightful plant on your windowsill. It is a low plant and so it should be planted near the front of the bed.

Thyme (*thymus vulgaris*)

There are probably more old legends and stories connected with this herb than any other. Wild thyme has always been a favorite with the fairies. It is said that if you wipe your eyes with it you can see them.

Bees always hover over the thyme plants, and an old herbalist told us that "the owner of Hives have a perfite foresight and knowledge what the increase or Yeelde of Honey will bee everie yeare by the plentiful or small number of flowers growing and appearing in the Thyme about the summer solstice."

Add to this a quotation from "Midsummer Night's Dream":

> *"I know a bank whereon the wild thyme blows,*
> *Where oxlips and the nodding violet grows;*
> *Quite over canopied with lush woodbine,*
> *With sweet musk roses and with Eglantine."*

We have a low bank of wild thyme at the back of our herb garden, in addition to an eglantine hede. As one passes by, the aroma is so lovely it is impossible to describe. If you plant creeping thyme along the crevices of a terrace, this same aroma will come to you as you tread upon it.

There are many varieties of thyme. We have 10 of them in our garden, which is only a beginning. I believe there are some 200 varieties in all. It might be fun to make a collection of your own thyme plants. They are a hardy perennial, though in northern climates it is best to hill them up with earth for winter protection. As a house plant they are charming. You cannot resist touching them and getting the haunting fragrance on your fingers every time you pass by.

Thyme vulgaris has a woody, fibrous root. The stems are numerous and branched, with many tiny, dark green leaves. It grows four to eight inches high. These tiny leaves are high in volatile oils, which give it its flavor for cooking. Use it in meats, stews and soups. Thyme can be seeded outdoors and thinned out when the plants are one inch high. Again, I would advise the beginner to buy a few plants. Thyme dislikes excessive moisture, so be sure to plant it in full sun. The creeping varieties will grow in places that are too hot for grass.

4

Herbs to grow in the shade

DON'T BE DISCOURAGED if you have only shaded areas for growing. Even though we are told that herbs need much sunlight, there are certain types that will grow in the shade. These plants may not grow as large as those in full sunlight, but they will be large enough to give you flavor and fragrance. The following list is worth trying:

Perennials

Burnet (*poterium sanguisorba*). Grows about six inches high, has a flavor of cucumbers.

Chives (*allium schoenprasum*). Onion flavor, grows about 12 inches high. Always cut off stems from the bottom of the plant, rather than shearing off the top. The plant will grow thicker if you do this.

Curly Spearmint (*mentha spicata*). Use for flavoring fruits and cold drinks; makes an excellent tea. Grows about two feet high, is apt to spread all over the flower bed. Suggest planting in large tin cans to keep roots in check.

Lemon Balm (*melissa officinalis*). Use for making tea and to flavor cold drinks. Has a strong lemon flavor. Will grow up to three feet, except in the shade.

Lemon Thyme (*thymus serpylium var. citriodorus*). Use for flavoring of all kinds, and for tea. Grows six inches high.

Lovage (*levisticum officinalis*). Has a celery flavor; use wherever that flavor is desired. Grows three to four feet high in the shade. (The leaves and stems will also be softer when grown in the shade.)

Tarragon (*artemisia dracunculus*). Use to flavor chicken, salads, soups, stews, and for tarragon vinegar. Grows two feet high. Be sure not to cut it until the plant is well established.

Wild Marjoram (*origanum vulgare*). Will grow straggly in the shade, but has a good flavor for meats, soups, stews, mushrooms.

Here are two perennial herbs that are not necessarily for cooking, but which can be used for ground covers in the shade:

Ground Ivy (*nepeta hederacea*). Has light, round, green leaves and a light, lavender flower in the early spring. It will grow in either sun or shade; in fact, it is hard to keep in check. In the early days the leaves were used to flavor ale.

Sweet Woodruff (*galium odoratum*). Has dark, glossy, green leaves and is covered with small, white, star-like flowers for six weeks in the early spring. The dried leaves smell like new-mown hay. It is the plant the Germans use for making the Maie Bowl. They call it "waldmeister."

Annuals

Basil (*ocimum basilicum*). Will not grow as well as in the sun, but will give some flavor.

Chervil (*anthriscus cerefolium*). Grows low, has flavor of anise. Use in salads and omelettes; make successive plantings.

Parsley (*petrosalinum crispum var. neapolitanum*). Use more as a food than just as a garnish. Sprinkle it with onion salt, and eat as we do radishes or celery. It is high in vitamins A and C.

Peppergrass (*lipidum sativum*). Grows about six inches high, has a strong, crisp, peppery taste; good in salads.

Rocket (*eruca sativa*). Grows about eight inches high, but will not stand upright without support. Has strong taste of peanuts; use leaves in sandwiches, with mayonnaise.

An abbreviated kitchen reference

	Appetizers	Fish	Meat	Vegetables
Basil	Vegetable and seafood cocktails	Shrimp, broiled fish	Stew, hash, meat loaf braised meat	Tomatoes, peas, beans, cucumbers
Chives	Veg. cocktails cheese spreads	Seafood salads	With sauces, in hamburgers and meat loaves	Mashed potatoes
Marjoram		Broiled fish, baked fish	Roasts, stews and meat loaves	Zucchini, spinach, mushrooms, potatoes
Savory		Broiled fish, baked fish	All meats, game, stuffing	Beans, cabbage
Tarragon	Fish and veg. cocktails	Broiled fish, shellfish	Meat, game, chicken	Peas. tomatoes
Thyme	Veg. cocktails	Stuffing	Croquettes, stuffing and meat loaves	Peas, carrots, onions

Shade and sunlight herbs for flavoring

Chives (*allium schoenprasum*). Perennial; no salad complete without this.

Chervil (*anthriscus cerefolium*). Annual; use in salads, soups omelettes.

French sorrel (*rumex scutatus*). Perennial; use the young leaves in salads, and for sorrel soup.

Garlic chives. Perennial, have delicate flavor of garlic; use in salads.

Parsley (*petrosalinum crispum var. neapolitanum*). Use as a food, not as a garnish. Eat like a salad; try sprinkling with onion salt.

Summer savory (*satureja hortensis*). Annual; use in salads. A must for string beans.

Sweet marjoram (*origanum marjorana*). Annual; used as a seasoning in creamed soups, meat and salads.

Sweet basil (*ocimum basilicum*). Annual; use to season any tomato combination and any fish.

Thyme (*thymus vulgaris*). Perennial; for use in salads, soups, creamed soups and flavorings of all kinds.

Tarragon, French (*artemisia dracunculus*). Perennial; use in salads, meats, soups, vinegar. Do not cut until plant is well established.

Rosemary (*rosmarinus officilanis*). Perennial, but not hardy in north. Use on meat before roasting and for flavoring soups. Use leaves in deep fat when frying potatoes.

Lovage (*levisticum officinale*). Perennial, grows to four feet high; has strong flavor of celery. Use in salads, soups, vegetables, wherever a celery flavor is desired.

5

A companionate guide

EVERYTHING WORKS BETTER when raised and used in the right company, and herbs are no exception. The following is a guide to where the most commonly used herbs feel most at home, and what their habits are when paired with a complementary mate.

Herb	Companions and effects
Basil	Companion to tomatoes. Dislikes rue intensely; improves growth and flavor, repels flies and mosquitoes.
Beebalm	Companion to tomatoes; improves growth and flavor.
Borage	Companion to tomatoes, squash and strawberries. Deters tomato worm; improves growth and flavor.

Camomile	Companion to cabbages and onions; improves growth and flavor.
Catnip	Plant in borders; deters flea beetle.
Caraway	Plant here and there; loosens soil.
Chervil	Companion to radishes; improves growth and flavor.
Chives	Companion to carrots; improves growth and flavor.
Dead Nettle	Companion to potatoes. Deters potato bugs; improves growth and flavor.
Dill	Companion to cabbage; dislikes carrots; improves growth and health of cabbage.
Fennel	Plant away from gardens; most plants dislike it.
Garlic	Plant near roses and raspberries. Deters Japanese beetles; improves growth and health.
Horseradish	Plant at corners of your potato patch to deter potato bugs.
Hyssop	Deters cabbage moth. Companion to cabbage and grapes; keep away from radishes.
Lamb's-Quarters	This edible weed should be allowed to grow in moderate amounts in the garden, especially in corn.
Lovage	Improves flavor and health of plants if planted here and there.
Marigold	The workhorse of the pest deterrents. Plant throughout garden; it discourages Mexican bean beetles, nematodes and other insects.
Marjoram	Here and there in garden; improves flavor.

Mint	Companion to cabbage and tomatoes. Improves health and flavor; deters white cabbage moth.
Pot Marigold	Companion to tomatoes, but plant elsewhere in garden; also deters asparagus beetle, tomato worm and general garden pests.
Nasturtium	Companion to radishes, cabbage, and curcubits. Plant under fruit trees, deters aphids, squash bugs, striped pumpkin beetles; improves growth and flavor.
Peppermint	Planted among cabbages, it repels the white cabbage butterfly.
Pigweed	One of the best weeds for pumping nutrients from the subsoil, it is especially beneficial to potatoes, onions, and corn. Keep weeds thinned.
Purslane	This edible weed makes good ground cover in corn.
Rosemary	Companion to cabbage, bean, carrots, and sage. Deters cabbage moth, bean beetles and carrot fly.
Rue	Keep it away from sweet basil. Plant near roses and raspberries; deters Japanese beetle.
Sage	Plant with rosemary, cabbage, and carrots. Keep away from cucumbers; deters cabbage moth, carrot fly.
Southernwood	Plant here and there in garden. Companion to cabbage; improves growth and flavor, deters cabbage moth.
Sowthistle	This weed, in moderate amounts, can help tomatoes, onions and corn.
Summer Savory	Plant with beans and onions. Improves growth and flavor, deters bean beetles.

Tansy	Plant under fruit trees. Companion to roses and raspberries; deters flying insects, Japanese beetles, striped cucumber beetles, squash bugs, ants.
Tarragon	Good throughout garden.
Thyme	Here and there in garden, deters cabbage worm.
Wormwood	As a border, it keeps animals from the garden.
Yarrow	Plant along borders, path, near aromatic herbs; enhances essential oil production.

This information was collected from many sources, notably from the Bio-Dynamic Association and The Herb Society of America. (Reprinted from *The Rodale Herb Book*, Copyright © 1974 by Rodale Press, Inc. Permission granted by Rodale Press, Inc., Emmaus, Pa. 18049.)

6

Herbs for decoration

FEW PLANTS MAKE such satisfactory or beautiful arrangements as herbs. Most people think herbs are used only for fragrance, flavoring, or medicine, and never for decoration only. How wrong they are. Using herbs for background foliage with flowers, or in combinations with themselves, makes pleasing arrangements.

At a past meeting of The Herb Society of America, then held in New York, a charming arrangement of herbs placed in a low, circular container or an ivy ring was displayed (a small clump of ivy, next to that sweet lavender, then violets, sage, wild rose, a sprig of rosemary, camomile, mint and thyme). This is perfect for a low arrangement in the center of the dining room table and starts a conversation piece among guests who want to learn the symbols of each plant. The rosemary is for remembrance, the rose for love, sage for health, violets for humility, sweet lavender for luck, thyme for courage, mint for cheerfulness, camomile for patience, and the ivy is a symbol of God.

Fern leaf tansy (*tanacetum vulgare crispum*) has a lovely, dark green, much-cut-into textured leaf. It resembles an ostrich plume in the way it rises from the stem with a deep curve. This curve will keep its shape when standing in a vase of water, and the plume-like leaf will keep fresh for 10 days. It is a hardy perennial that spreads rapidly every year.

Another interesting herb for arrangements is perilla (*perilla frutescens crispa*). This plant is a beautiful deep, garnet red color. It is an annual but seeds itself so readily that once planted

Knot garden at New Jersey's Well-Sweep Farm shows herbs in delicate pattern of colors and aromas.   Photo by Hollis Keats

in the garden it will appear in many places the following year. Arrange this in a vase with pink snapdragons or any other pink flower that blends well with this deep red color. It is stunning.

Purple basil (*ocimum basilicum purpureum*) has a dark brown color with purple tinges, and this too, used with a pink or lavender, is lovely and has a delightful aroma.

Most refreshing of all are the mints, which can be used with any combination of flowers. They stand perky and fragrant in water for over a week. New flowers can be added to the arrangement as the old flowers fade, thus making it last for a good bit of time.

When it comes to the grey herbs, there are many that can be used to great advantage, and of course their fragrance is very pleasant. Southernwood (*artemisia arbeotanum*) is a tall, soft, feathery grey plant that mixes well with any color of flower.

Silver mound artemesia (*artemesia schmidtiana nana*), also a perennial, is just what its name implies — a silvery, very soft, feathery plant. One cannot resist leaning down to touch it. A cool-appearing arrangement for a hot day can be made by using the dark green, fern leaf tansy laid flat around the edge of a low dish with the center filled with the soft, grey down of the ar- temisia silver mound.

Lemon Balm (*melissa officinalis*), a hardy perennial, has a small, round, light-green leaf that makes nice arrangements.

Be sure not to cut your herb plants in the late fall. The tops, when left on, give a certain amount of winter protection, and some of them will turn beautiful brown colors. These can be picked in winter to use in dried bouquets.

There are many other herbs that can be used for flower arrangements. The ones mentioned here are easily grown, are usually not attacked by pests and need little or no fertilizer. They need only a friable soil and plenty of sunshine.

Herbs in tubs or pots for the terrace

A good project is growing herbs in tubs or pots on your terrace or porch. Rosemary can be used for a high focal point on the two ends of a terrace, after it has grown to a height of two or three feet (which it will do, after a few years' time). Rosemary is not hardy in northern climates, so it should be brought inside during the winter. It makes a lovely house plant.

A low tub, painted to match its surroundings, can be planted with creeping thyme, lemon-variegated thyme or creeping camomile, and this can be used for a seat. Can you imagine anything more delightful than to sink onto a soft seat of thyme or camomile and be surrounded with the delicious aroma that these plants will exude when sat upon?

Silver mound artemisia (*artemisia schmidtiana nana*) makes a beautiful round, soft, silvery ball, for another accent. This is hardy and can be left outdoors all winter.

Basils are always decorative, especially the purple varieties. Snips of this can be cut off all summer to use for flavoring any tomato or fish dish. Try a combination of the silver mound artemesia in the center of a pot and the dwarf purple basil around the outer edges. This is a beautiful combination. The basils are annuals, and hence should be seeded right in a pot.

For a shady place, try sweet woodruff (*galium odoratum*). Its little, white star-shaped flowers will bloom in the early spring and last for six weeks. In a round tub it will give the effect of a large, white pin cushion when in bloom.

The more venturesome can try a small design made of teucrium and santolina. The dark green of the teucrium and the light grey of the santolina make a fine mix. The beauty of this is that it will keep green all summer.

Any of the fragrant geraniums and lemon verbena are especially good to have on a terrace near chairs, where their delicious fragrance can be enjoyed. These too must be brought into the house for the winter, as they are not very hardy.

Even though you may not have space for a herb garden, you can still have herbs by growing them in pots or tubs on a porch or terrace. This feature makes the pleasures and uses of herbs available to anyone willing to invest a little time and effort.

For the kitchen windowsill, when winter comes

Fall is the time of year to gather in and plant herbs for use and enjoyment during the winter months. In the old days, the lady of the house was expected to be an authority on herbs "for the greater comfort of her household." Unfortunately, little knowledge of the herbs remains. For those willing to experiment, there is much satisfaction in growing a few herb plants in a sunny window.

If the kitchen has such an area, try to grow some of the herbs that can be used in cooking. It will be good to have them nearby, where a snip of this and that can enhance the flavor of your food.

Basil (*ocimum minimum*), the low variety, called bush basil (whose name is from the Greek, meaning king), has been used for perfume and flavoring since early times. If you already have a plant of this in your garden, pot it up before danger of frost and bring it indoors. If you do not have a plant, start a seed, which will germinate in 12 days, and as soon as the leaves are large enough to pick, use them for seasoning. They are especially good in flavoring any kind of tomato or fish dish.

Chervil (*anthriscus cerefolium*), is a fine annual that will germinate from seed in 12 days. As it does not stand transplanting, place the seed in the pot in which it is to stay. Chervil is a feathery cousin of parsley and in some ways is a more attractive garnish than parsley. This plant does not need as much sun as other herbs, and likes plenty of moisture. Place all potted plants on a saucer on which pebbles have been scattered, and keep the pebbles moist at all times. Chervil has an anise flavor and is especially good in omelettes and salads.

Chives (*allium schoenprasum*) are a hardy perennial and are best started from a clump of bulbs or from a plant brought in from the garden. They multiply quickly and should be cut often to keep them tender.

Dill (*peucedanum graveolens*), an annual, is grown commercially for its seeds (which are used in the manufacture of gin). Dioscorides, in the 1st century A.D., maintained that "ye decoction of ye dried haire and of ye seed being drank . . . stayeth ye hickets" — maybe reason enough to grow them as an antidote to an excess of gin. Dill grows quickly and must be cut frequently. The leaves are used to flavor many dishes, especially in French casseroles and beef Stroganoff.

Oregano is from the Greek, and means, "joy of the mountain." It is well-named, for it gives such pleasure to those who merely touch it and are rewarded by its enchanting fragrance.

Thyme (*thymus vulgaris*), a hardy perennial, is one of the old-time herbs and is used today to a far greater extent than ever before. It grows slowly, so for a window plant it would be best to buy a plant unless you have one to transplant from the garden.

Try these few herbs to use on a sunny kitchen window. They are well worth growing and will more than repay you for your efforts.

Decorating for Thanksgiving — a time for sage

The use of herbs at Thanksgiving time is probably more important than any other season of the year. How could we have our turkey without a dressing — and how could we make that dressing without sage (*salvia officinalis*)! It is one of the oldest and better-known of the herbs. It's not a native with us; its natural habitat is the northern shores of the Mediterranean, where it has been cultivated for culinary and medicinal purposes for many centuries. The name, salvia, is derived from the latin, *salvere* (to be saved), in reference to the curative properties of the plant. "He that would live for aye, Must eat sage in May," was one of the old proverbs.

Gerard, the well-known herbalist, said: "Sage is singularly good for the head and brain. It quickeneth the senses and memory, strengtheneth the sinews, restoreth health to those that have the palsy, and taketh away shakey trembling of the members."

The Chinese preferred sage tea to their own native product; at one time they bartered for it with the Dutch and gave three times the quantity of their choicest native tea in exchange.

Sage is a hardy perennial in the Midwest, though it is apt to die out after four or five years. At that time, new plants must be started, either by cuttings or seed. Sage keeps its color all through the winter, so it can be harvested anytime, though the leaves are at their best for fragrance and flavor just before flowering time (in early July). Cut the branches, hang them to dry in an airy attic or closet, and place in a covered jar when the leaves are dry enough to crumble.

A combination of a teaspoon of dried sage and a teaspoon of dried mint makes an excellent beverage. Place the herbs in a china, glass or enamelware teapot (never a metal one), and pour two cups of boiling water over them. Let steep for five or 10 minutes, strain, and flavor with honey and lemon, never cream or sugar.

In decorating your Thanksgiving table, take a cabbage and spread out the leaves to make it look like a large rose. Use this for the center of the table, placing it on a pewter or tin grey tray, if possible. Lay bunches of green grapes, lemons and limes, interspersed with rue, to elongate the design. In two separate vases, at either end of this arrangement, use small yellow chrysanthemums with rue for the background foliage, which will pick up the grey of the cabbage.

Rue will keep in water indoors for several weeks, and is lovely in any flower arrangement with its soft, lacy texture. "Herb o' Grace," Shakespeare called it. It is a hardy perennial, starting readily from seed. The leaves can be cut into small pieces and mixed in cream cheese balls, which adds a tart taste. The French used to lay it among clothes to keep the moths away, calling it "Garde Robe."

Also, try a "Tussie-mussie" by the plate of each guest. This is a little fragrant bouquet that can be pinned on and enjoyed for the rest of the day, and then laid away amongst handkerchiefs or linens where it will impart its fragrance for over a year. Tussie-mussies can be made by combining dried, fragrant leaves of the rose geranium, sweet marjoram, thyme or rosemary (any of which make good house plants that can be used all winter).

Christmas — the season for rosemary

Memories of the excitement and mystery of childhood Christmases can be conjured up by certain scents. The preliminary aromas of Yuletide begin with the pre-holiday baking, when the spicy vapors of anise seed in cookies, cinnamon and ginger in fruit cakes and citron and cardamon in coffee bread fill the house. This is the time of year when we fill the house with the nostalgic scents of Christmas greens as we decorate with pines, holly and balsam, and herbs.

The herb that ranks first among all others at this time of year is rosemary. The name means "dew of the sea," and the plant, growing naturally near the sea, always has the smell of the ocean as well as a tangy, aromatic fragrance of pines. It is a perennial, and although not hardy in northern states it can be brought

Herbal border garden shows variety of shapes and sizes.

Photo by Hollis Keats

indoors to make a good house plant. Keep it in a sunny window and water it sparingly; spray often with a water mist.

One legend tells us of the Virgin Mary in her flight from Egypt with the Christ child. She spread her cloak over a bush, which happened to be rosemary, and ever after the flowers were tinged with blue, caught from the blue of the cloak. Around Christmas time these flowers bloom up and down the stems of the plant, and one feels the legend has come true.

The ancients were well acquainted with the rosemary shrub, which had a reputation for strengthening the memory. On this account it became the emblem of fidelity for lovers; hence the quotation from Shakespeare: "Rosemary, that's for remembrance." Not only was rosemary used at weddings, but also for decorating the halls and churches at festivals, and especially at Christmas time.

A rosemary plant will make an unusual little Christmas tree, with single red cranberries and tiny blue bells hung for decoration. Little else is needed for ornaments; the plant's grey, silver and green boughs are quite decorative by themselves.

In making Christmas wreaths, be sure to tuck in bunches of rosemary. These will keep their color and fragrance for months, as do so many of the herbs used this way.

How many people know the taste of a rosemary wine or cordial? Rosemary tea is delicious. Rosemary as a culinary herb glorifies meat, poultry, sauces, greens and stuffings. Try it for flavoring your Christmas cookies, to give them just that special touch.

A rosemary plant is a good one in your home, where its fragrance and beauty can be enjoyed and its legends help give us the real meaning of Christmas.

The gifts of the three wise men were "gifts of the garden." Frankincense was obtained from the gum or resin of Boswellia carterii. Myrrh was a fragrant gum, probably from the rock rose (*cistus landaniferus*). In early times the shepherds obtained it by combing the fleece of the flocks. It is the sweetest of scented substance. Some goats were allowed to run through the bushes and then it was combed out from their beards.

So let us go back to the herbs at this time of year, reading their legends and stories, and renewing our faith and hope in these "Christmas Eve Thoughts from an Herb Garden":

> *"Twas pennyroyal bloomed that night*
> *The angels came to earth.*
> *And o'er the stall at Bethlehem*
> *Proclaimed our Saviour's birth.*
>
> *"And thyme was on sweet Mary's bed,*
> *To bring her courage rare,*
> *While shepherds lifted up their hearts*
> *In silent, joyful prayer.*
>
> *"And now in fond remembrance of*
> *That night so long ago,*
> *I add this sprig of rosemary*
> *To keep his love aglow."*

7

The fragrant herbs

ONE OF THE pleasures of an herb garden is the variety of scents that can be used from these sweet-smelling plants. Herbs have long been used to freshen the air, make perfumes, scent candles and soaps, and lift the spirit. Scented cosmetics and household products are easy to make and provide hours of fragrant pleasure. And when summer fades, the treasures of herbal scents can be stored in herb wreaths and sachet bags.

Handcrafting various herbal products is an enjoyable hobby. I find it intriguing to start with a few handfuls of dried herbs and turn them into useful, scented cosmetics and household arrangements. A potpourri jar, for example, makes a cherished gift.

Sweet basil and lemon balm were the very first herbs I grew many years ago and are now two of my favorites. I grow 150 varieties of scented herbs that find their way into my home and life in a variety of useful and fragrant ways.

Potpourris and sachets have long been favored ways to capture the scent of aromatic herbs. Huge urns of dried fragrant herbs were used by the Romans to perfume the air; Greek women often tucked small sachets in their gowns. Except for consistency, potpourris and sachets are almost identical. Potpourris are composed of coarsely broken bits of herbs, spices and flowers, while sachets are powdered mixtures.

Potpourris are displayed in decorative ceramic or clear glass jars that have tight-fitting lids. To make one, mix all ingredients in a large bowl; add oils last, and blend carefully. Put the mixture in a large glass jar with a tight lid and store in darkness for two months. Once a week, open the jar and stir. When finished, place in potpourri jars or, for sachets, grind before filling bags. Here are a few suggestions:

Lavender rose jar
- 2 cups rose petals
- 2 cups rose geranium leaves
- 2 cups lavender flowers
- 1 cup rosemary
- ½ oz. orris root
- 8-10 drops lavender oil

Lemon blend
- 3 cups lemon verbena leaves
- 1 cup dried lemon peel
- 1 cup lemon balm
- 2 cups bergamot flowers
- 1 cup thyme
- ½ oz. orris root
- 10-12 drops lemon oil

Herb oils may be purchased in herb and botanical shops or you can make your own from a bumper crop of herbs or roses. Try a drop of herb oil behind your ear — it is superb perfume.

Extracting oils from aromatic plants requires time and many fresh flowers or herbs. Fill a ceramic crock with the scented herb of your choice (lavender blossoms, mint leaves, rosemary, thyme or rose petals are good choices). Gently press the botanicals down and cover them with either rain or spring water. Set the crock outdoors in full sun, moving it only if rain is likely. In about a week an oily film should appear on the surface. With a small piece of cotton carefully soak up the precious oil and squeeze it into a small bottle. Cover with a tight-fitting lid.

Homemade soaps and candles may be enlivened with herbal oils. Soap is easy to make — merely follow the directions given on most brands of household lye. Prior to pouring it into molds, add several teaspoons of the essential oil to it. Scented oils such as rosemary, citrus mint or lemon are good choices for either soap or candles. Add oils to candles made of paraffin or beeswax once the wax is melted, and just before pouring it into molds.

Herbal baths can turn bathing into an aromatic, soothing experience. A leisurely herbal bath relaxes muscles and scents the body with garden fragrances. To prepare one, use one of two methods: 1) place a large handful of herbs in a piece of cheesecloth and tie this under the faucet so that water runs over the bag as the tub fills, or 2) simmer a bunch of scented herbs in one gallon of water for 10 minutes, then strain and add this scented water to that in the tub. Remember that herbs may be used alone or in combination. Favored bath herbs include camomile, calendula, lovage, rosemary, lavender, mint, thyme and lemon balm. Lavender calms frayed nerves; sage relieves sore muscles; comfrey and rose petals help rejuvenate the skin.

Bath powders are the perfect ending to an herbal bath. Powder two ounces of rosemary, lemon thyme or bee balm and stir into two ounces of cornstarch. To fix the scent, add several teaspoons of powdered orris.

Breath fresheners need not come from the corner drugstore. Sweeten your mouth by slowly chewing a leaf of peppermint or spearmint, or munch on a few anise seeds. Another method is to hold a whole clove in your mouth for a few minutes. This is an ancient practice. And to clear "garlic breath," chew parsley.

Herb wreaths look — and smell — attractive on doors or over mantles. Place a generous amount of dried wormwood or silver king sprigs lengthwise on an eight-inch by 36-inch piece of two-inch mesh poultry netting. Roll up edgewise and fasten the cut edges together by bending the wires. Form the resulting 36-inch-long tube into a circle and secure the ends to each other. Decorate this base generously with thyme, oregano, rosemary and winter savory. For accent, add rose hips, basil seed stalks and rue seed pods. For color, add tansy blooms, yellow or pink yarrow umbels. Finish with a colorful bow.   —*Bonnie Fisher*

8

The Williamsburg gardens

Virginia's Colonial Williamsburg — the marvelously successful effort of one man to reach out and provide us all with a living window into our American history — was awakening to another summer day. It was my first visit to the gardens of the George Wythe House, the apothecary shop and the John Blair House — herbal gardens that represent part of the colonists' daily interests in health, table fare and color of their trappings.

Unlike vegetables, herbs have grown, been used and passed on to others in an unaltered state since 2,000 B.C. We know this from the *Ebers Papyrus*, which mentions about 2,000 herb doctors in Egypt, any of whom could probably recognize the herbs in one of today's gardens.

The three herbal gardens of Colonial Williamsburg are within easy walking distance of one another. One is the Pasteur-Galt Garden behind the apothecary shop on the Duke of Glouchester Street, near Raleigh Tavern. It has herbs representing the organic-medicinal era. The other two gardens are home herb gardens. One is beside the George Wythe House on Palace Green, adjacent to Bruton Parish Episcopal Church. Behind it

Photo by Francis Sheild

lies a vegetable garden. The third is a knot garden on the John Blair House property, which faces Duke of Gloucester Street next to the Bruton Parish residence house. All three are operated on a free-admission policy.

"These are gardens set as they may have been in the 18th Century," says Bob McCartney of Williamsburg's landscape staff. "With the Apothecary Shop here you would assume there was a relationship between the garden and the shop." And so it was. The proximity of medicinal and culinary gardens here shows the importance of these miracle plants in the day-to-day lives of our ancestors. It was only a few steps from the kitchen to the garden for a pure-grown seasoning or cure. This was the original inflation-proof store of seasonings and medicines.

"Most herbs are native of the Mediterranean area and like a climate that is considerably drier and sunnier than we have here," says McCartney. "Some of the herbs grow under what we call almost desert conditions. A lot of people in hot, humid areas mistakenly try to grow their herbs in the shade of trees and buildings, where there is a root competition from trees, and poor air circulation. This causes a lot of problems. The best location is out in full sun in a well-drained place that gets good air circulation."

Records of early days in Williamsburg show that apothecaries of the 18th century relied on imports from Europe or the Orient for much of their medicinal trade. This inventory was then supplemented by herbs collected from the wilds and then replanted domestically. The latter means gave them a steady supply and an advertisement of their stores.

The Pasteur-Galt Garden site was acquired in about 1760 by Dr. William Pasteur, city surgeon of Williamsburg. He paid 200 British pounds sterling, and four days later resold parts of it to merchants, keeping the center section for his apothecary and surgery shop. This he operated for approximately 18 years. In 1775 Dr. John Galt returned from study in Edinburgh, Scotland, and joined Pasteur. In 1778 Pasteur sold out to Galt for 1,650 pounds sterling.

With an eye to archeological findings, the narrow little apothecary shop was reconstructed with outbuildings in 1950, restoring the street to the era of Pasteur. Now when you visit the garden behind the shop on a summer day, you can see the

Photo by Francis Sheild

common herbs once used here, and now reinstated for exhibit: Sweet William, Chinese pink, hyssop, Roman Chamomile, sage, cowslip, fennel flower, chives, sweet basil, common marjoram, gray santolina, various thymes, rosemary, costmary, lemon balm, elfwort, coriander and lovage.

Another part of the Williamsburg gardens west tour is the George Wythe House. Wythe was first professor of law in the United States and instructor of Thomas Jefferson, James Monroe and Henry Clay, as well as a member of the committee that prepared the Constitution. His house served as General Washington's headquarters during the Yorktown campaign and is one of the 80-odd buildings that survived the colonial period to be restored as one of Williamsburg's open exhibition buildings. A self-sufficient unit, it was equipped to receive and store supplies from outlying plantations. The centrally placed bowling-green garden is now lined by handsome sassafras trees. The herb garden is in the first four blocks along the left wall, together with the house's vegetable garden, and contains the usual simples and pot herbs common to home use.

The knot garden of the John Blair House faces Duke of Gloucester Street. It is reminiscent of 17th century design, and the narrow brick-bordered walks divide the 40' x 50' area into two diamond-shaped beds. This garden is cleverly well-maintained with herb plantings that are revised from year to year: golden chamomile, lavender, garden parsley, rosemary, thyme, catnip, spearmint and Oswego balm. It lies next to the main house, home of John Blair (an associate justice of the Supreme Court), and his 10 children. This house was one of the first restored by Williamsburg's initial program in 1929. If you pause to look over its picket fence some summer day, the smells of the garden and the authentic reconstruction of the village can lure your imagination two centuries back in time. Like the rest of Colonial Williamburg's gardens, the herb collection will inspire you to prize your history.

—*Francis Sheild*

9

Herbal remedies

"The Lord hath created medicines out of the earth, and he that is wise will not abhor them."   —*Ecclesiastes*

SOMETIMES IT SEEMS modern doctors have taken away from us the comforts of old-time remedies. How good the camphorated oil rubbed on the chest used to feel, along with hot cloths applied to the throat. And how many of us have sat before a steam kettle breathing in the vapor of tincture of benzoin? All this seems to be a thing of the past. We are now given pills that accomplish remarkable cures, to be sure, but still some of us hanker for those old-time comforts and the safe, uncomplicated remedies they used to bring.

Natural medicines continue to draw increasing interest, perhaps due to a wary public attitude of the side effects of synthetic pills and drugs. The applications of herbs to cure common ailments are many, as detailed here, and although we encourage the study and use of medicinal herbs, we caution the neophyte against careless use.

Dill, often mistaken for fennel, and a favorite workhorse in kitchen use, is a good remedy for curing swelling and pains. It flourishes best in well-drained soil and full sunlight.
Photo by Hollis Keats

Marion Wilbur, for example, is hesitant to reveal many of her herbal remedies, explaining that they may have harmful effects if they aren't used properly. Says she: "Herbs are powerful plants. For many of them, you have to know what you're doing." A list of some uses to which she puts certain common herbs is shown below. If the enterprising herbalist is interested in trying these cures, caution should be used, especially with those herbs to be taken internally. Marion's suggestions:

- Betony (*Stachys officinalis*) can be steeped or applied as a poultice to aid in the healing of ulcers and superficial cuts, respectively.
- Borage (*Borago officinalis*) is commonly imbibed as an exhilarating tea, as well as an aid in easing rheumatism.
- Scotch Broom (*Cytissus scoparius*) can be drunk to counteract jaundice and bladder ailments. (Wild buckwheat, *erigonum*, can also be used.)
- Burdock (*Arctium lappa*) is a valued salve for curing several skin diseases such as boils, burns, scurvy and eczema.
- Foxglove (*Digitalis purpurea*) has been used to stimulate the heart (but that should remain as evidence of history, not as a guide for practice).
- Goat's Rue (*Galega off.*) is used to lower blood sugar in diabetics and as an agent to increase lactation in cows.

- Henbane (*Hyoscymus*) is a powerful poultice that relieves pain of gout and similar discomforts.
- Lemon Balm (*Melissa off.*) is said to discourage bee stings when rubbed on the skin, and promotes sleep when taken as a tea. If a bee does sting you, a poultice of marshmallow (*Althea off.*) will relieve the pain.

- Most of the members of the mint family make delicious teas and produce general soothing for digestive disorders.
- Mugwort (*Artemesia vulgaris*) is also good for indigestion, as is Silky Wormwood (*Artemesia frigida*).
- Mullein (*Verbascum phoeniceum*) is said to cure deafness when taken internally, and is also a mild sedative.
- Purselane (*Portulaca oleracea*) is used internally against ulcers and externally to promote healing of hemorroids.
- Pellitory-of-the-Wall (*Parietaria off.*) is commonly used as a remedy for bladder stone and many urinary problems.
- Queen Anne's Lace (*Daucus carota*) is useful to counteract gout.
- The young shoots and roots of the Sea Holly (*Eryngium maritimum*) have nerve-tonic properties and aid in soothing chest ailments when they are eaten.
- Infusion of the Teasel root (*Dipsacus fullonum*) aids in stomach and liver complaints.
- The root of the Yellow Dock (*Rumex crispus*) is said to be a mild tonic for chronic skin diseases.

In addition to these remedies, there are several gentle and soothing ointments that can be made simply and used to relieve sore muscles and refresh the bath. An aromatic rubbing mixture can be made as follows: Cover the herbs below with warmed rubbing alcohol:

2 oz. sage leaves
2 oz. rosemary leaves
1 oz. lavender flowers
½ stick of cinnamon
2 oz. balm leaves
2 oz. peppermint leaves
½ oz. fennel seed

Place this mixture in an airtight container for several days, then filter and dilute with one-half part water.

The following are recipes of mine that are taken from the old books; try them or not as you think fit. We have had some remarkable cures with the few we have tried in our family.

Peppermint (*mentha piperita*) is a hardy perennial that flowers in late summer. This, when "boiled in milk and drunk hot," is good for abdominal pain.

Common yarrow (*achillea millefolium*) grows plentifully in our fields and along roadsides. Yarrow tea is a good remedy for severe colds, "being most useful in the commencement of fevers, and in cases of obstructed perspiration." In cases of a severe nosebleed, its leaves, crushed and applied to the nostrils, will stop the flow of blood. "It has the reputation of being a preventive of baldness if the head be washed with it," some ancients have said.

Horehound (*marrubium vulgare*) is for colds and coughs. Make a tea by pouring a pint of boiling water on one ounce of the leaves. Let it steep for 10 minutes, strain, and take a wineglass full three or four times a day.

Honey posset (for insomnia)

One of the best preventives for insomnia is honey, provided you are one of those with whom honey agrees. Place a third of a pint of milk in a saucepan to which a tablespoon of honey has been added, and stir this over a flame until the honey has melted. Add the strained juice of a lemon or grapefruit, and drink just before retiring.

For those suffering from asthma, try putting an ounce of dried lemon thyme into a muslin bag and fasten it to the pillow.

Parsley tea

This was a noted old-fashioned cure for rheumatism and arthritis. To make it, put a good handful of parsley, including stems, into a pint of cold water. Bring slowly to a boil and let simmer gently half an hour. Drink half a pint twice a day.

Inhalants

When an attack of either asthma or bronchitis threatens, the inhaling of some preparation that will stay the irritation is desirable. The following are said to be excellent:

Friar's Balsam — Get a small quantity of balsam from a chemist. Put a teaspoonful into a jug containing a pint of boiling water. The sufferer should hold his head over the jug and breathe the steam, first covering his head with a towel.

Burning Coffee — Here is a useful inhalant that is at hand in most households and is especially useful if an attack comes on in the middle of the night when quick relief is required. Put a heaped tablespoon of dry coffee into a spoon and set a lighted match to it. As a rule, there is no difficulty in getting the coffee to ignite. As it burns it gives off an aromatic smoke that will generally relieve fits of coughing and difficult breathing. For that purpose it is as good as the pastilles generally employed in commercial medicine.

Burning Camphor — For the same purpose, a small piece of camphor may be employed in a similar manner. On the first experiment it is better to choose a very small piece of camphor, as it will burst into flame at the touch of a lighted match (but will soon burn itself out harmlessly).

Common plantain — Usually considered an obnoxious weed that many saturate with a poisonous spray to get out of their lawns. In reality it is one of the most astringent herbs that grows. A Dutch woman visiting our garden told us that she had fallen through a dyke when a child, badly lacerating one leg. The doctor wanted to amputate, but her mother refused to let him do so. She applied poultices of plantain, and the leg was saved.

One day I cut my finger on a tin can. The finger became infected and, remembering the story of the Dutch girl, I picked a leaf of plantain, put it under very hot water and wrapped it around the infected finger. In 24 hours the pain had gone and the infection had subsided.

Another plant that we have used with great success is celandine (*chelidonium majus*), a cure for warts. Break the stem and apply the yellow acrid juice to the wart two or three times a day. After a few weeks the wart should disappear. This is a very painless remedy when compared with the doctor's needle.

An herb with considerable healing characteristics is aloe. To promote scar-tissue healing, or to soothe burns, break one of the tubular stems in half and force the plant's glue-like juice over the wound. One plant, which normally grows a half-dozen long-stemmed leaves, should be good for a year's worth of scraped elbows, skinned knees, kitchen burns, etc.

Even better than aloe, claims Marion Wilbur, is a mixture of one-third horsetail-and-vinegar brew with two-thirds raw milk. Horsetail grows wild along creek beds, and was discovered as a natural healing inducement mix by a British veterinarian who disliked chemical-oriented medicines for animals, and set out to research old-time cures. Eventually she found frequent mention of the horsetail mixture, and with practice and a little experimenting, brought it back into use.

"It's a lot more convenient to use than aloe," says Marion, "mainly because I keep it in a little squirt bottle. This makes it easier to apply. And I think it heals faster."

We have used winter savory (*satureia montana*) to cure itching skin. Bruise the leaves and rub on the affected parts. You will get almost instant relief.

Summer savory (*satureia hortensis*) is good for a bee sting. Bruise the leaves and rub them on the sting, and keep doing this for a few minutes. The relief is almost instantaneous and there is no swelling.

The pity of it all is that the knowledge of herbs has been lost, to a great extent. When I tell someone of these cures they usually laugh. Fortunately there are exceptions, such as my friend who was stung by one of my bees. We rushed to the herb garden where I immediately administered summer savory to her lip. It seems she was planning to go to a very special party that night, and all she could think of was a swollen and disfigured lip. She was perfectly amazed at the relief the summer savory gave her, and also that her lip did not swell up later on. She said to me the next day, "Did I ever have a conversation piece that night!"

Herbs are powerful, so know what you're taking

Although we are excited about the curing power of herbs and other natural plants, using them for medicinal purposes involves two problem areas: sales outlets where labeling and quality are improperly monitored, and imprudent use by persons who are not familiar with the plants in question. Simply put, uninformed use of herbs can be dangerous. To sober even the most enthusiastic herbalist, let us conclude this chapter with segments of an Associated Press story that ran in many newspapers on

August 5, 1979. It is written by AP science writer Kevin McKean and is reprinted here with permission:

NEW YORK (AP) — " . . . Herbs escape careful scrutiny by the Food and Drug Administration because they are rarely labeled as drugs. Yet many herbs contain ingredients the FDA would require a prescription for, or might ban if they were sold as drugs. Some herbal books and magazines tout them as cures for everything from the common cold to cancer.

"Trade groups concede it's hard to police the quality of herbs because of mislabeling or adulteration with other products.

" 'I would say it's chemical roulette,' says Ara H. Der Marderosian, a botanical pharmacologist at the University of Pennsylvania.

" 'If it's available on a retail shelf, most citizens believe someone has scrutinized this material for safety, or it would not be there,' says Walter H. Lewis, a botanist at Washington University in St. Louis.

"David Ajay, president of the National Nutritional Foods Association, estimates the health food business has grown tenfold in the last decade and now rings up annual sales of $500 million. It is a movement founded, he says, on people's suspicions that processed foods are not nutritious enough to keep them healthy.

"But physicians and botanists say naturalness is no guarantee of safety."

10

Substituting herbs for salt

LEARNING TO USE sweet herbs in place of salt is healthy and provides an array of new taste experiences. Certain herbs can enliven and enhance the flavor of food, thereby reducing or even eliminating the need for salt.

Research has suggested that the vast amount of salt consumed by Americans is largely responsible for hypertension (high blood pressure) and edema (water retention), and the shortened lifespan due to these ailments. In countries where salt consumption is low (averaging 1.5 to 3 grams daily) there is a corresponding low incidence of hypertension. In non-salt-using societies the average daily consumption from natural sources is 800 milligrams, whereas the average American intake is four to six grams (about six times more).

Besides that which is added in cooking or later at the table, salt is invariably used as an inexpensive ingredient in prepared foods. Additionally, many food additives are sodium-containing compounds. A few examples show the staggering amount of salt found in some favorite prepared foods: three ounces corned beef — 1491 mg. salt; one cup creamed cottage cheese — 560 mg.

salt; one ounce American cheese — 332 mg. salt; one hot dog — 499 mg. salt; three ounces potato chips — 840 mg. salt; one large dill pickle — 1924 mg. salt; one tablespoon baking powder — 1230 mg. salt.

Sodium is a necessary nutrient that keeps normal fluid levels in body cells and maintains the health of the muscular, nervous and blood systems. However, the body's need for sodium is usually met by foods naturally rich in this nutrient. Individuals who eat a diet rich in meat and dairy products consume plenty of sodium as all meats, poultry, fish and milk contain high levels of this nutrient. Most fruits, vegetables, greens, grains and legumes also contain sodium. Celery and carrots are especially rich sources as are parsley, spinach and chard.

Cutting down on the consumption of sodium chloride, better known as table salt, can be accomplished in one of two ways. The easier route for most palates is by gradually reducing added salt over a period of two to six months while using more herbs. Eliminating all added salt at once is more difficult but also may be done by relying on herbs and the natural flavor of foods. I gradually used less salt and more herbs over a period of time and now very rarely salt anything.

Besides adding interest and flavor to food, culinary herbs contain vitamins, minerals and trace minerals. Most herbs are good sources of vitamins A and C, as well as iron.

If herb cookery is new to you, go light in the beginning — add just a pinch. Begin with the mild, sweet herbs first. Include some basil in the tomato soup; add dill weed to a tossed salad; sprinkle chicken with paprika; spice up the lima beans with a touch of savory. Like all food and flavorings, herbs are an acquired taste. Experiment and find out your preferences. Go easy in the beginning, especially with the stronger tasting herbs such as sage, rosemary and curry.

Add herbs about 10-20 minutes before a dish is done. Overcooking destroys the flavor, but a small amount of cooking is required to release the essential oils and allow them to saturate the dish. Always use lids so the flavorful oils don't escape into the air. Either fresh or dried herbs may be used in the kitchen. As dried herbs are more concentrated, use about one-quarter the amount as when using them fresh.

To insure the freshest possible flavor in dried herbs, store them in tightly covered glass jars. As heat and light destroy flavor and color, try to store them in a cool location out of direct sunlight. Herbs over one year old tend to lose or change flavor.

Herbal salts and substitutes

Herbal salts may be used to fill the salt shaker and are handy to keep near the stove. Begin with top-quality dried herbs. Remove any stems and browned leaves, then grind the remainder to a fine powder in an electric blender, or by using mortar and pestle. Sift to remove any large pieces. These powders may be used to fill the traditional salt shaker or may be mixed half or more with either table salt or sea salt.

Powdered sweet marjoram and oregano are both fine salt substitutes. A powdered blend of equal parts celery leaf and thyme is another savory choice. And a small amount of curry powder or chili powder is a welcome addition to this blend. Another all-purpose blend is equal parts sweet marjoram and rosemary with a touch of cayenne (use either alone or mix blend two-to-one with sea salt). One more taste-bud pleaser is three parts each of thyme and parsley to one part each sage and curry powder. These above powdered herbs, used either alone or blended with salt, will enhance egg and cheese dishes, salad dressings, stews, soups, vegetables, dips and all meat and poultry dishes.

Fill another of your salt shakers with "Gomasio," a Japanese seasoning of sea salt and sesame seeds. Begin by lightly roasting raw sesame seeds in a dry skillet over low heat for two to five minutes, stirring often. Grind a small amount at a time to a fine powder in an electric blender before mixing with sea salt. The proportion of sesame seed to salt can be as little as 1:1 or as much as 4:1.

Powdered kelp (a seaweed) is another good salt replacer. Although kelp contains sodium, its content is 1/23rd that of table salt (one tablespoon salt contains 6962 mg. sodium, compared to 300 mg. for one tablespoon kelp). Use kelp in place of salt. It looks like pepper, but has a distinct, light salty taste.

Selecting the right herb

As a rule, the stronger, more aromatic herbs make the best salt replacers. My favorites include bay leaves (used to form a background flavor in combination with a stronger herb such as rosemary or sage), celery (both the leaf and seed), chili powder, coriander seed, cumin seed, curry powder, dill weed and seed, fennel seed and leaf, garlic (the more the better), sweet marjoram, mint, oregano (a favorite), paprika (sweet, mild taste and rich in vitamins A and C), parsley (loaded with vitamin C), rosemary, sesame seed (good protein source), sweet basil, sage, summer savory, tarragon (essential to French cuisine) and thyme.

Here are suggested salt replacements, listed by food categories:

Herbal salt substitutes

With: Use:

SOUPS

With:	Use:
Borscht	Thyme, dill
Bean soups	Savory, cumin, garlic, chili powder
Chicken soup	Tarragon, rosemary, thyme, sage
Chowders	Fennel, thyme, sage
Pea soup	Rosemary, mint
Soup stock	Bay, thyme
Tomato soup	Thyme, basil, oregano
Vegetable soup	Savory, thyme, oregano

EGGS & CHEESE

With:	Use:
Cheese sauces & dishes	Basil, dill, sweet marjoram, mint, parsley, sage, tarragon, curry powder paprika
Omelette & scrambled eggs	Celery, dill weed, sweet marjoram, oregano, rosemary, sage, sesame seed, tarragon
Souffles & quiches	Parsley, thyme, rosemary, chili powder, basil, oregano

With: Use:

MEATS

Beef & veal . . . . Bay, celery, chili powder, dill weed,
sweet marjoram, oregano, paprika,
rosemary, sage, thyme

Lamb . . . . Bay, celery, curry, tarragon, sweet
marjoram, garlic, coriander, oregano,
parsley, rosemary

Pork . . . . Sage, bay, dill, sweet marjoram,
paprika, garlic

POULTRY

Chicken & turkey . . . . . . Bay, sweet marjoram, sage, paprika,
oregano, basil, thyme, sesame, tar-
ragon, savory

Goose & duck . . . . Bay, sweet marjoram, sage, rosemary

SEAFOOD

Fish . . . . Tarragon, dill, fennel, paprika, basil,
thyme, sweet marjoram, mint,
parsley, sage

Shellfish . . . . Dill, oregano, rosemary, tarragon,
fennel, thyme, paprika

SALADS

Cole slaw . . . . Dill seed, celery seed, fennel,
oregano, paprika, mint, sesame

Fruit salads . . . . Mint, rosemary, sweet marjoram,
fennel

Green (mixed) . . . . Basil, celery, coriander leaf, dill
weed, fennel greens, garlic, mint,
parsley, tarragon, sesame

Potato salad . . . . Dill, parsley, sesame, savory, celery

Tomato salad . . . . Basil, thyme, dill, savory, celery

Vegetable salads . . . . . . Basil, parsley, thyme, savory, celery

With: Use:

VEGETABLES

Beans & legumes .... Savory, thyme, cumin, coriander, sesame, tarragon, sage, parsley

Carrots & squash ...... Basil, bay, dill, sweet marjoram, parsley

Cooked greens .... Celery, mint, parsley, sesame, coriander, cumin

Green vegetables (all)... Sweet marjoram, parsley, sesame, oregano, rosemary, sage, thyme

Potatoes.............. Celery, cumin, dill, fennel, garlic, sweet marjoram, oregano, paprika, parsley, thyme, sesame

Rice, eggplant, mushrooms, tomatoes..... Thyme, basil, savory, oregano

DRESSING & SAUCES

Dips .... Dill, parsley, garlic, mint, thyme, savory

Gravies.............. Bay, basil, sage, thyme, chili powder, paprika

Marinades .... Bat, tarragon, thyme, rosemary, celery, dill, garlic, oregano

Salad dressings .... Paprika, dill, thyme, oregano, basil, tarragon, sesame, fennel, garlic, celery, curry, sweet marjoram

White butter sauces .... Basil, dill, sweet marjoram, parsley, thyme

BREADS & DESSERTS

Breads & rolls .... Dill, Oregano, celery seed, paprika, sesame seed, fennel seed

Cookies & cakes .... Sesame seed, fennel seed, dill seed, coriander seed

—*Bonnie Fisher*

Dorthea Nobeck of Wisconsin readies dried herbs for tea.

Photo courtesy of Organic Gardening magazine

11

Recipes

ONCE YOU'VE USED herbs, food tastes flat and uninteresting without them. Caution must be taken in using seasoning, however, for if too great a quantity is used, it is far worse than none at all. Herbs should be used sparingly, sprinkled on food like seasoning, just before serving, or heated in a pan with vegetables or meats for the last few minutes of the cooking period.

Before the days of iceboxes, meats were often wiped with herbs to help keep them fresh. Herbs were also used for flavorings and seasonings. They took the place of vegetables, which were not a part of the bill of fare until a few hundred years ago.

When you use herbs, you are getting your vitamins in their natural form, in the way they can best be assimilated by the human body. This is a far sight better than getting your vitamins in synthetic doses, as when taken in pill form. Parsley, for instance, has more vitamin A than most cod liver oils, and more vitamin C than a similarly weighted volume of orange juice. During the First World War, children in England were given parsley tea to take the place of orange juice, which was frequently unobtainable. In this country we have been accustomed to using it merely as a garnish. Try eating it just as you would radishes.

Herbs are classified under three main headings: medicinal, fragrant and culinary. It is with the latter group that this chapter is primarily concerned: how to use them for seasoning. This text includes recipes of tasty and simple dishes, in addition to several old New England recipes taken from my mother's and grandmother's cookbooks. My mother had a way of affixing to the recipe card the name of the person from whom it came, and as I look back on these names I am reminded of my childhood days spent on a farm in New England. "Lizzie Edwards' Chocolate Pie," for instance, is one good memory. Lizzie used to cook for the farm hands. She was a plump, jolly woman who was always clad in a blue-and-white striped calico dress, buttoned tightly all the way down across her bosom. Her black hair was parted in the middle, and slicked down to a bun pinned at the back of her head. She used to blow a tin horn to call the men to meals. One day, after the chickens had been killed for eating, we children filled the horn with feathers. When she came to blow it, out flew the feathers in a white cloud! Lizzie was left spluttering and gasping for breath. She was a great character and a superb cook.

Many of the recipes included here are known only to our family. I share them here in the hope that you will enjoy them as much as we have.

Editor's note: Except when credited otherwise, these are the author's own recipes. We suggest that before starting on any one of them, you first read it through *entirely*. This way you won't discover that you were supposed to have already sautéed the onions *before* adding them to the stew . . . Such planning may help prevent anxiety attacks. Happy cooking.

Soups

WHEN YOU CONSIDER THAT soup was so important two centuries ago that a soup tureen was on nearly every table and a traveler carried soup with him on a journey, it is hard to understand why it is used relatively little nowadays. Soups of the old days were hearty, made often of beef, well-seasoned with vegetables and herbs. Of course we have to remember that these soups were made over coal fires where they could simmer on the back of the stove for hours, and so their flavors were delicious and they were very nourishing. It's a lesson of sorts to try some of these old recipes, so different from what we have now:

An onion soup, call'd The King's Soup

"Take some onions cut in very thin Slices, stew them till tender, in small Quantity of Water, then add Milk, let it boil together, at least half an Hour, with a pretty many Blades of Mace, and a quarter pound of fresh Butter; a little before it is taken up, thicken it with Yolks of two Eggs well beaten, and some Parsley, pick'd and chopp'd very small; salt to your Taste: Serve it with Toast cut in Dice."

About four large onions to two quarts of milk.

—The Lady's Companion, 1753

N.B.: Make your own soups with the blender, using whatever is on hand, including leftover vegetables. But remember that two or two-and-a-half cups of liquid is necessary, be it milk, juice or water. Soup stock can always be substituted by using two beef or chicken bouillon cubes with two cups of water.

A basic cream soup consists of:

2½   cups milk, or 1¼ cup milk and 1¼ cup cream
2   tbsps. butter
1   tsp. salt, a few dashes of paprika
1   cup raw or uncooked vegetables
      Season with herbs, a pinch of marjoram, thyme and tarragon.

Chilled tomato soup

Beat one cup of milk and one cup cream with one can tomato soup. Add a sprinkling of sweet basil and chives. Place in refrigerator until ready to serve. Can be served hot or cold.

Pea Soup

1   cup fresh green peas, or frozen peas
1   tbsp. diced onion, dash of pepper
2½   cups seasoned chicken broth
2   tbsps. butter
¼   tsp. dried mint

Place all ingredients in container of blender or food processor, in order indicated. Cover container and turn on blender. Run until peas are well blended, about one minute. Pour blended mixture into saucepan and bring to boil, stirring constantly. Makes four servings.

Leek Soup

Melt one tablespoon butter in a sauce pan. Add five or six sliced leeks and turn for five minutes until soft and golden. Add one scant quart beef bouillon, one slice stale bread, salt and pepper and simmer until leeks are quite tender. Strain and serve with garlic croutons.

Garlic Croutons

Cut white bread into cubes. Fry two sliced cloves and garlic in four tablespoons butter. Remove garlic and fry bread cubes in butter. Add to the soup at the last moment.

—The Herb Grower Magazine, Isabella Gaylord

Watercress Soup

One large handful of watercress. Wash it well, cut up roughly, and toss into a blender. Sprinkle over it one tablespoon of flour, plenty of salt and pepper and add a pint of chicken broth and a cup of heavy cream. Then break in two fresh eggs, and blend for a couple of minutes. Remove, and cook in a double boiler for about half an hour.

A few croutons, made by frying tiny squares of whole wheat bread in garlic butter, can be added. Garnish with a couple of the nicest watercress leaves.

Pumpkin Soup

2 lbs. pumpkin
   Remove seeds and pare off rind

Cut in small pieces and put in stew-pan with one-half pint water. Simmer slowly for 1½ hours. Rub through a sieve and put on the stove with 1½ pints of boiling milk, a lump of butter the size of an egg, one teaspoon sugar, and salt and pepper to taste.

Stir occasionally, and when it boils, serve. Cans of pumpkin can be used instead of cooking fresh pumpkin, if so desired.

Vegetable Soup Made in Blender/Processor

1   cup water
2   beef bouillon cubes
1½ cups tomato juice
¼   tsp. dried sweet basil
¼   tsp. lovage, dried
¼   cup diced raw onion
½   cup sliced carrots
     small bunch of parsley

Place all ingredients in container of electric blender (food processor), in order indicated above. Cover container and turn on blender. Hold cover on. Run until ingredients are partially blended (about two seconds). Pour blended mixture into saucepan and bring to boil. Let simmer over low heat for about 10 minutes. Correct seasoning if necessary. Serve immediately. Makes four servings.

Lizzie Driscoll's Cream of Lettuce Soup

Take the tender part of two heads of lettuce and chop finely. Fry a little chopped onion in a tablespoon of butter, being careful not to burn it. Add two tablespoonsful of rice, then the lettuce, and cook for a few minutes in the frying pan. Have two quarts of chicken stock ready. Put this all on to boil for one-half hour or until the rice is cooked. Then add one cup of scalded cream and, finally, the beaten yolks of three eggs. Season with salt and pepper and serve at once (or it will curdle).

French Sorrel Soup

2 handfuls sorrel
4 tbsp. butter
2 or 3 egg yolks stirred into 1 cup cream or milk
2 cups boiling water or chicken stock
1 tsp. flour. Salt and pepper to taste

Wash and dry sorrel. Chop it finely and cook in butter until it becomes pulp. Sprinkle in flour, salt and pepper; add chicken stock or boiling water and cook 20 minutes. (Chicken stock or bouillon cubes are the best.) Put all this in the blender for a few seconds. Beat egg yolks and cream together and add to the mixture when it is cool (otherwise the eggs will curdle). Heat just before serving, but do not boil.

Tomato Soup for Canning

This is an excellent recipe to use at the end of the season, just before a heavy frost, when all that will freeze in the garden must be picked and used.

1   bushel tomatoes
16   large onions
8   large stalks celery
12   green peppers
2   cans okra (or fresh okra if you have it)
1½ cups sugar
1½ cups salt

Start with one tablespoon sweet basil, dried, or a handful of the fresh. Peel tomatoes, put peppers and onions through meat grinder; cut celery into fine pieces. Boil all together for one hour. Seal in jars. This makes 21 quarts. With crackers or croutons added, it can make a luncheon dish for a cold winter's day.

Western Chili

1 lb. ground beef
1 green pepper, chopped
4 cups tomatoes, chopped
1 bay leaf
3 tbsps. chili powder
1 tsp. paprika
2 cups kidney beans, cooked

Brown beef. Stir in pepper, tomatoes and bay leaf. Simmer for 30 minutes. Add remaining ingredients and cook another 15 minutes. Serves four to six.

Black Bean Soup

1 cup black beans, cooked
2 quarts stock
1 onion, chopped
1 clove garlic, minced
½ tsp. rosemary
½ cup brown rice
¼ cup sesame seeds

In large saucepan combine beans and stock. Bring to simmer. Add onion, herbs and rice. Cover and cook until done.

Zesty Potato Soup

4 potatoes, chopped
2 cups stock
2 cups milk
1 tsp. sweet marjoram
1 tbsp. parsley, minced
1 clove garlic, minced

Cook potatoes in stock until soft. Purée in blender. Return puréed potatoes to stove and stir in milk. Heat through. Stir in herbs. Serves four.

—Above three recipes from Bonnie Fisher

Buyshala

A yogurt soup with several variations, this soup is delicious cold or hot. It comes from northern Iran and Turkey and is also popular among the yogurt-loving people of the Caucasus. It can be made when herbs and green vegetables are plentiful, then canned for winter.

Mix together in a large four quart pot:

1   egg
2   tbsps. flour
1   cup yogurt

Add:

½   cup rice, barley or yellow split peas
3   cups water
4   cups yogurt

Place over medium heat and cook until grain or peas are ready (about 20 minutes). Then add:

1   cup shredded cabbage
½   cup chopped celery, leaves and stems (optional)
1½ cups chopped fresh or 1 cup frozen spinach
1   cup chopped Italian parsley
2   cups chopped Swiss chard, stems and leaves

Cook until the greens are tender. Turn off heat. Stir in ½ cup chopped coriander leaves. Cover the pot and let stand for 10 minutes. Salt to taste and serve hot or cold or can in jars without wax. Serves eight.

—Eden Frye

Chilled Tomato-Dill Soup

6   large, ripe tomatoes
¼   cup dill sprigs or 1 tbsp. dried dill weed
1   cup water
1   cup heavy cream
1   cup sour cream
     salt and pepper to taste

Dip tomatoes into boiling water for 30 seconds; remove and peel. Core and halve them horizontally. Remove and discard seeds. Place tomato pulp into blender or food processor with dill and water. Blend at top speed until smooth. Pour into a bowl and stir in heavy cream and sour cream. Season to taste with salt and pepper. Chill for several hours. Serve topped with additional dill sprigs. Serves six.

—Sarah Farwell

Salads

"In Health, if Sallet Herbs you can't endure,
Sick, you'll desire them, for Food or Cure."

—*Old Proverb*

"We present you a tast of our English garden Housewifry in the mater of Sallets. And though some of them may be vulgar [as are most of the best things] yet we impart them to show the Plenty, Riches, and Variety of the Sallet-Garden. And to justify what has been asserted of the possibility of living (not unhappily) on Herbs and Plants according to Divine institution."

—*John Evelyn, Acetaria, 1699*

How to make a salad

WHENEVER POSSIBLE, MIX THE salad in a wooden bowl. Cut a section of garlic and wipe the bowl gently with it. Place the lettuce leaves and other greens in the bottom of the bowl. Do not mix the dressing on the leaves until just before serving. Cut the herbs in fine pieces with scissors (or scatter the dried herbs). If you are grating vegetables, do likewise. A simple salad dressing is one part vinegar or lemon juice to three parts oil, seasoning with salt and pepper and a pinch of sugar. Mix the vinegar with the seasonings over the leaves first, then add the oil. The oil coats the leaves, and it is impossible for the lemon juice or vinegar to penetrate them if put on first.

In using herbs, remember to use them sparingly: one teaspoonful of finely cut fresh herbs or one-quarter of the dried herbs for four servings of vegetable, meat, fish or salads. Be guided by your own taste. Some like salads more highly seasoned than others. In using sweet basil or sweet marjoram in a salad, one leaf of each is sufficient. They have a strong flavor and would dominate the whole if used in too great a quantity.

Dressings

Lemon juice is sometimes substituted for vinegar. A wine vinegar is sometimes preferred to a malt vinegar. The latter is harsher and very acid.

French Dressing

1 tbsp. wine vinegar
3 tbsps. olive oil
½ tsp. salt; ground pepper, equivalent of few shakes; one pinch sugar
3 drops Worcestershire sauce. Add finely chopped tarragon, chervil, savory or fennel
1 tsp. of an herb, or combine any desired.

Salad dressing without oil

To three parts of sweet condensed milk add two parts vinegar or lemon juice and season to taste. To a quarter-pint of the mixture add half a teaspoonful of mustard. Pour the milk in a bowl, add the seasoning and mustard and mix well. Add the vinegar or lemon juice, very slowly, beating well. Add a teaspoon of chopped chives. If vinegar is used, this dressing can be bottled.

Sour Cream Dressings

1. Take one cup of sour cream beaten with one tablespoon of lemon juice or vinegar. Season with paprika, a sprinkling of lovage leaves and chopped chives.
2. One cup sour cream, one salt spoon salt, one tablespoon fresh tomato juice, one tablespoon lemon juice. Beat all of these together.

There are many interesting combinations that can be made with sour cream. Experiment with it and make some of your own. Sour cream is always a welcome addition to vegetables and meats when warming over dishes.

Country chive dressing

¾ cup mayonnaise
3   tbsps. vinegar
2   tbsps. honey
¼   cup fresh chives, minced

Blend well. Keep refrigerated. Use on salad greens.

—Bonnie Fisher

Trida

A cold yogurt soup with several variations, this is a versatile dish that may be served as a soup, a dressing for salad or vegetables like broccoli, or watered down and served as a refreshing summer drink. Stir together the following:

1   pint plain yogurt
2   cups finely chopped cucumber
¼   cup finely chopped dill (it must be fresh)
¼   cup finely chopped coriander leaves (fresh)
2   tbsps. chopped chives, scallions or shallots or a combination

Salt to taste. As soup it serves four persons. (One cup chopped walnuts and raisins may be added. If mint is preferred, use ¼ cup peppermint and omit the dill and coriander.)

—Eden Frye

In the early Spring, many wild greens can be used in salads. These are the good old-fashioned blood purifiers. They are very tasty and can be mixed together in a salad bowl and a French dressing can be added to them. The following list are all edible and good, in small quantities: mustard, chicory, wild onion, pepper grass, curly dock, horseradish, purslane, cowslips, dandelions, lamb's-quarters, violets (sprinkle the flowers over all after the French dressing is on), plantain, watercress, sheep sorrel, Good King Henry, and milkweed sprouts.

Mixed Green Salad

Break, but do not cut, a variety of salad greens such as romaine, escarole, chicory, lettuce, dandelion leaves, sorrel leaves, young Swiss chard leaves and watercress into a salad bowl. Add sliced cucumber, onion rings, green peppers, radishes, quartered tomatoes. Season with salt and dress with herb French dressing (below).

Carrot Salad

Grate five carrots, snip small handful of chives with scissors, add a pinch of tarragon if dried, add a few snips if it is fresh. Then add one tablespoon raisins; mix these in one tablespoon mayonnaise, and mix all with carrots. Place small bunches of parsley around the dish (on which you should sprinkle a little onion salt).

Carrot and Apple Salad

Follow preceding recipe, then grate three apples, skins and all; add more mayonnaise dressing if it seems too dry. Garnish with bunches of parsley.

Beet Salad

Grate five good-sized beets. Mix sour cream dressing all through them. Serve on platter with lettuce or parsley.

Cabbage Salad

Grate cabbage, add a few pinches of dried tarragon and lovage to mayonnaise; also add one teaspoon chives, then salt and pepper to taste. Mix the dressing all through the cabbage. Add a few slices of apple, and some nuts.

Tomato and Celery Salad with Herbs

1 whole good-sized tomato per person
3 leaves head lettuce
1 tblsp. finely diced celery
1 tblsp. finely cut-up apple
1 tsp. mayonnaise dressing in which a generous pinch of sweet basil and chives have been mixed
Salt and pepper to taste.

Halve tomatoes and scoop out pulp after they have been peeled; chill in refrigerator. Mix herbs with mayonnaise, celery and apple. Stuff tomatoes with mixture and serve at once. Fresh herbs in variety from the garden may also be used, such as summer savory, chervil, or tarragon.

Lime and Cucumber Salad

1 medium-sized cucumber; quarter it and remove seeds
1 small onion
1 cup mayonnaise
1 cup almonds
1 package lime jello
1 cup cottage cheese
¼ tsp. chives; pinch of summer savory and tarragon

Put cucumber, onion and almonds through meat grinder or processor. Melt lime jello in three-fourths cup boiling water, let cool. Mix cottage cheese and other ingredients with mayonnaise. Add jello, stir all together and put in a mold. Serve on a large platter, surround the mold with lettuce leaves. Shrimps, crab meat and tomatoes can be added on top of the lettuce, if a heartier dish is desired. Serves 12.

Savory Bean Salad

3 cups green beans, cut in 1'' pieces and cooked
3 hard-boiled eggs, chopped
2 sweet pickles, diced
1 carrot, grated
½ cup mayonnaise
½ tsp. summer savory
  fresh parsley

Stir together vegetables and eggs. Toss with mayonnaise and savory. Garnish with parsley.

Potato Salad

6 potatoes, boiled in jackets and chopped
1 carrot, chopped
2 stalks celery, chopped
1 scallion, chopped
½ cup mayonnaise
4 hard-boiled eggs, chopped
1 tsp. dill weed
¼ tsp. celery seed

Combine vegetables and eggs. Stir in remaining ingredients. Serve chilled. Will serve six.

—Above two recipes from Bonnie Fisher

Herb French Dressing
(*Variation No. 1*)

One cup salad oil, one-third cup tarragon vinegar, one clove garlic bruised, one teaspoon chives or grated onion, one teaspoon sugar, one-fourth teaspoon paprika, one teaspoon salt, pepper (a few shakes), one teaspoon dried mixed herbs, or one teaspoon each of fresh basil, tarragon, chervil, lovage, summer savory and parsley. The latter should be cut up in fine pieces with scissors. This dressing will keep for some time.

Caesar Salad

This is hearty enough for a luncheon course or for a Sunday night supper. Fry two cups white bread cubes and one minced garlic clove in butter to make golden crisp croutons. Set aside to drain on paper towels until salad is completed. Tear up a large head of romaine lettuce and put in a salad bowl. Sprinkle with one-half teaspoon dry mustard, one-half teaspoon salt and black pepper, one-half cup grated parmesan cheese.

Over this pour the juice of one large lemon and six tablespoons olive oil. Soft-boil two eggs for a scant minute; break them over the salad and toss it very thoroughly. Add croutons, toss again briefly, and serve at once. Do not let this stand or the croutons will get soggy — they should be very crisp.

This is a good dish for herb growers as you may experiment with various herbs. Since there is cheese, perhaps a little sage; since eggs, basil or tarragon; since garlic, a bit of parsley. Use about one-half teaspoon of each in the fresh, finely chopped form.

Herb-and-Honey Dressing

Mrs. Webster, in her book of herbs, "How to Use Them and Grow Them," tells of a herb-and-honey salad dressing given her by the late Mrs. Bratenahl:

For the usual green salad of endive, lettuce and chicory, dissolve one-fourth cake comb honey in the juice of one lemon. Combine with one cup salad oil and herb vinegar (two tablespoons). Add paprika and salt to taste, then add a pinch of celery seed.

Beat or shake until quite well-mixed and then add cut-up leaves of chives, lovage, burnet, sorrel and perennial onion leaves that have been cut crosswise, so that they make little thin circles. This should be a sweet dressing so thick with herbs that it must be ladled, not poured. It is delicious when blended thoroughly with green salad leaves. (Rub salad bowl with garlic beforehand.)

‚Tossed Green Salad

Take two heads of lettuce, a bunch of watercress and any other greens obtainable. Wash greens and dry them thoroughly before mixing with the dressing. Scatter through the leaves the following herbs: chives, summer savory, lovage, tarragon, garlic chives. Make a simple French dressing (see first recipe); pour this over leaves and mix the dressing into the salad.

Mayonnaise dressing: for cooked vegetables, mayonnaise should be thinned with cream.

Tomato mayonnaise: Make a puree of uncooked tomatoes, mix with a little cream and add one teaspoon chopped basil to mayonnaise.

French Dressing Variation No. 2

1	can tomato soup
¾	cup vinegar
1	tsp. salt
½	tsp. paprika
	A few grinds of black pepper (the freshly ground pepper is always best)
1	tsp. sweet basil
1	tbsp. Worcestershire sauce
1½	cups oil (olive oil or peanut oil if possible)
½	cup sugar
½	tsp. dried mustard
1	tsp. onion juice

Put all together in a jar and shake well. Add one clove garlic and leave that in the jar. Always shake well before using.

Dressings for Cucumbers

Slice cucumbers, sprinkle with salt, let stand one-half hour. For each person add one tablespoon sour cream that has been flavored with chives. Pour this on cucumbers, surround with tomatoes that have been sprinkled with sweet basil and flavored with a little onion salt.

Russian Dressing

½	cup mayonnaise
¼	cup chili sauce
1	tsp. minced chives
½	tsp. summer savory
½	tsp. basil

Salads such as these give you your vitamins in their true form. You can make all kinds of combinations; do not be afraid to do so. Try grating raw turnips, Jerusalem artichokes, potatoes, cabbage, carrots or any other kind of raw vegetables. Vary your dressings and flavors with the herbs. If you have a liquifier or blender (and if you don't you should surely get one) you can make your own mayonnaise dressing in three minutes time. This dressing can also be varied by adding tomato ketchup, or chili sauce, or a few drops of Worcestershire sauce, chives, onion juice and various herbs.

Fish

MY FATHER, WHO PASSED away in 1956, once told me this:

"The finest chafing-dish oyster stew that ever tempted a jaded appetite is made by an ebony deity who presides over the kitchenette of an uptown New York bachelor, who imported this treasure from Virginia (where he was chef in one of the hotels that prides itself upon its fine old southern cookery). To make this ravishing tid-bit you have to use your own judgment as to quantities. The ebony deity we speak of declares that "diff'unt folks like diff'unt quantities, and dey has to suit deyselves."

Ingredients: oysters, chopped celery, a good deal of tomato catsup, Worcestershire sauce, a little mustard, pepper, vinegar and a little sherry to taste.

Tumble them all in and stew, stirring occasionally. Serve very hot with slices of toast and stalks of celery.

"Deelishus," says its inventor.

Prussian Perch

2	pounds ocean perch fillets
¼	cup yogurt
2	tbsps. vinegar
3	tbsps. onion, minced
¼	cup tomato juice
2	tbsps. vinegar
3	tbsps. onion, minced
¼	cup tomato juice
2	tbsps. dry milk powder
1	tsp. oregano

Place perch skin side down in shallow baking dish. Stir together yogurt, vinegar, onion, and juice. Blend in milk powder and oregano. Pour over fish. Baked 20 minutes at 350°F. Serves six.

—Bonnie Fisher

Salmon Slices

Buy small salmon slices. Flour them lightly and cook in generous amount of butter until slightly brown and about half-done. Add two wine glasses white wine and boil over a brisk flame until liquid is greatly reduced, but enough is left for a generous sauce. Put on a serving platter, cover with sauce and sprinkle with minced tarragon or basil.

—Isabella Gaylord, "Herb Grower" magazine

Finnan Haddie

Wash haddock, soak for one-half hour in cold water, skin side up. Drain and cover with boiling water and let stand five minutes. Drain again carefully. Remove skin and bones and place fish in buttered crumbs and bake in a hot (400°F.) oven long enough to brown the top.

Cream Fish in Fish Mold

3   lbs. halibut cooked about ½ hour, then flaked; chop whites of hard boiled eggs into fish
1½ cups heavy cream
3   tbsps. lemon juice
    dash cayenne pepper
1   tsp. salt

Combine, put in molds and bake 20 minutes.

Salmon Spread

1   can salmon, drained with all bones removed
½   cup mayonnaise
1   tsp. lemon juice
2   tsp. chopped chives, geraniums, or shallots
1   tsp. chopped parsley
1   tsp. chopped tarragon

Combine all ingredients; mound onto a plate and chill. Garnish with parsley heads and lemon balm leaves. Serve with wheat thins.

—Marcia Barber

Salmon Salad

1   lb. salmon
1   carrot, chopped
1   stalk celery, chopped
1   clove garlic, minced
½   tsp. dill seed
1   tbsp. oil
¼   cup mayonnaise

Flake salmon with fork. Combine all ingredients and stir lightly. Chill and serve on greens or use for sandwiches.

—Bonnie Fisher

Mrs. Edgerly's Escapped Lobster

Cut 5 lbs. lobster quite fine. Make a sauce of:
1 pint heavy cream
2 tbsps. butter
3 tbsps. flour, a speck of cayenne, salt and pepper.

Put cream on to boil. Mix butter, flour and pepper together, and add three tablespoons boiling cream. Stir into the remaining cream and cook two minutes. Add lobster, salt, more pepper, if needed, and boil one minute. Pour into a buttered escallop dish. Cover thickly with fine bread crumbs and butter; brown in a hot oven. (White stock will do in lieu of cream.)

Filet of Sole or Flounder

(Preferably sole, which has a slightly more delicate flavor.)

Buy as many filets as needed and wipe with a damp cloth. Grease a shallow baking dish with butter; lay the filets in and season them with salt and pepper. Sprinkle one teaspoon of dried rosemary or sweet basil over them and pour over enough cream to just cover the filets. Sprinkle thickly with parmesan cheese and top with chives, cut very finely. Cook in 475°F. oven for about 10 minutes, or until well browned. Serve immediately.

—Isabella Gaylord, "Herb Grower" magazine

Tuna and Noodle Casserole

Cook 18-oz. of medium-broad noodles in boiling water for ten minutes. Drain and put half in the bottom of a well-greased casserole. Sauté one-half cup sliced onions, one-third cup chopped green peppers, and one minced clove garlic in butter until garlic is golden. Add a can of mushroom soup, salt and pepper and pour one-half of it over the noodles in the casserole. Add one-half the onion mixture, half of a No. 2 can of tomatoes (or similar portion of frozen or fresh tomatoes) and half a can of tuna. Repeat the layer. Crush a small package of potato chips, but not too fine, and mix into them one-half teaspoon each of basil and marjoram. Bake at 400°F. for 20-35 minutes. This serves six generously.

—Isabella Gaylord, "Herb Grower" magazine

Dilled Salmon Steaks

Place salmon steaks in shallow buttered baking dish. Squeeze fresh lemon juice over them. Sprinkle them with crushed dill weed. Drizzle melted butter over the steaks and top each one with thinly sliced onion. Bake uncovered at 375°F. for 20-35 minutes.

Barbequed Swordfish

Marinate swordfish steaks in one-half cup melted butter or margarine, the juice of one lemon, and two tablespoons chopped chives for 30 minutes. Butter a sheet of aluminum foil and poke several holes in it. Place foils and fish in grill. Grill for 5-10 minutes each side, brushing constantly with marinade. Fish should flake easily when done. Serves two.

Herb-Stuffed Fresh Trout

Wash and dry cleaned trout. Squeeze juice of one-quarter lemon into each trout. Fill cavity of each fish with the following:

¼   tsp. each of fennel, lemon thyme, chives, garlic salt
2   chopped shallots
2   tbsps. chopped mushrooms
2   tbsps. chopped celery

Lay fish in shallow baking dish. Pour approximately one cup of white wine (or to taste) over them and dot each one with butter. Bake at 375°F. for 20 minutes or until fish flakes easily.

—Above three from Marcia Barber

Meat

"In the old days it was probably the shepherds who discovered different concoctions of meats, herbs and wild vegetables. At sundown, these lonely men would sit by their tripods with a kettle hanging over the fire, in which a wonderful brew had been simmering for hours."

IF NO HERB IS mentioned in the following recipes, try adding some. Any of the herbs listed below are good to add to meat dishes. Remember the amount — one-fourth teaspoon of the dried herb or one full teaspoon of the freshly cut (fresh ones are always better) to serve four people.

Use *tarragon* in any chicken dish.

Lovage where you want a flavor of celery.

Thyme in any red meats, especially meatballs.

Chervil gives a very subtle flavor.

Dill is good to sprinkle over lamb chops.

Sweet marjoram, sprinkled over veal chops, gives just that special flavor.

Summer savory can be used in any meat dish; so can *chives*.

Confetti Stuffed Chicken

2-3   slices whole wheat bread
½   cup sunflower seeds
1   onion, chopped
1   carrot, chopped
½   tsp. sage
2   cups tomato juice
1   whole chicken

Toast bread and cut into one-fourth inch cubes. Add sunflower seeds, onion, carrot and sage. Mix well. Stir in one-half cup tomato juice. Stuff bird and place in covered casserole. Pour one-half cup tomato juice over chicken. Bake at 375°F. one-and-a-half to two hours or until done. While baking baste two times with the tomato juice.

Curried Turkey

2   stalks celery, chopped
1   onion, chopped
3   tbsps. oil
¼   cup whole wheat flour
2-2½   tsps. curry powder
2½   cups milk
1½   cups turkey, cooked and chopped

Lightly saute celery and onion in oil. Stir in flour and curry. Slowly add milk to thicken. Add turkey and heat through. Serve on brown rice or whole wheat noodles.

Candied Apple Chops

4 pork chops
2 tbsps. oil
4 apples, sliced into rings
1 cup raisins
2 tbsps. honey
1 tsp. cinnamon

Brown pork chops on both sides in oil. Place one-half apple rings in bottom of greased baking dish. Sprinkle half of raisins over apples and then one-half teaspoon cinnamon. Lay pork chops over all. Use remaining apple rings to cover pork chops. Sprinkle with remaining raisins and cinnamon. Drizzle honey over mixture. Bake at 350°F. for one hour.

Bavarian Stew

1 lb. stew meat
1 qt. water
2 cups tomatoes, chopped
1 tsp. caraway seed
1 cup zucchini, chopped
1 onion, chopped
3 carrots, chopped
3 cups potatoes, chopped
1 cup yogurt

Brown meat in oil using large Dutch oven. Add water and simmer for one hour. Add vegetables and caraway and cook until vegetables are of desired doneness. Stir in yogurt just before serving. Will serve four.

—Above four from Bonnie Fisher

Turkey Tetrazzini

Cook one-half lb. spaghetti and put into a large casserole. Brown one-half lb. mushrooms, sliced, in four tablespoons butter or bacon fat. Add four tablespoons flour and two cups of turkey broth (or chicken bouillon made with a cube) and stir until smooth. Add one cup heavy cream and five tablespoons sherry, along with one-half teaspoon thyme and one-half teaspoon marjoram. Stir again until very well blended. Add three cups diced cooked turkey, chicken, or tuna meat, to the sauce; pour it over the spaghetti, sprinkle heavily with grated parmesan cheese, and set aside until one-half hour before serving. Brown in a moderate oven and serve piping hot.

Turkey Hash

Cut up the meat very finely. Stew the bones in a little water, strain, then stir meat into this water, adding a large tablespoon butter mixed with flour, a cup of cream, salt and pepper, a little chopped parsley, thyme or celery (or else a very few celery seeds). Stew all together.

—From an old Williamsburg Cook Book

Ham Dreams

Grind up two cups or more of cooked ham with one-half green pepper, one onion, one clove garlic, two hard-cooked eggs, one sprig tarragon, a few leaves of sage and two large sprigs of parsley. Mix well, fold in one tablespoon lemon juice and enough mayonnaise to bind well. Just before serving, toast four slices of bread on one side. Then remove from broiler, spread untoasted side heavily with ham mixture, put one tablespoon mayonnaise on top, sprinkle heavily with parmesan cheese and toast until golden brown. Serve at once, very hot.

Nora's Boiled Tripe

Wash tripe. Dry well with a towel. Then dip in milk. Have frying pan very hot; brown butter a little then fry tripe, a piece at a time, adding butter if needed. When all is cooked, put on a hot platter, add salt and pour melted butter over all.

Jennie's Chicken à la King

2 fowls, boiled and cut up
1 lb. mushrooms
1 pint cream
2 pimientos
salt and cayenne pepper
3 egg yolks

Cook the mushrooms in a frying pan with a little butter, until tender. Put cream in double boiler and when hot add cut-up chicken and cut-up pimientos. Then add mushrooms and just before serving add the yolks, well-beaten, and two tablespoons sherry. Serve on toast.

Warmed-over Roast Beef à la Union Club

Use English mustard, Worcestershire sauce and sweet oil, equal parts worked to a paste with a knife. Put on slices of beef cut from a roast (one-inch). Roll in bread crumbs and broil on a quick fire. Serve with a sauce made by thinning the paste with melted butter worked in with a wire whisk.

Shepherd's pie

Take cold roast beef, slice it thinly, cut in rather small pieces, moisten with gravy. Add salt and pepper and put it in a baking dish. Chop a small onion and put over the meat. Pour one cup stewed tomatoes over this, and over that pour some nicely mashed potatoes, well seasoned. Bake until the potatoes are browned.

Mutton Curry

Fry one tablespoon onion in one tablespoon butter. Mix one tablespoon curry and one teaspoon salt with one tablespoon flour. Stir into the butter and onion and gradually add one pint hot water or stock. Cut two pounds lean mutton into pieces, add to the sauce, simmer until tender and serve with a border of boiled rice.

Lamb in Mold

1 cup minced lamb
½ cup milk
2 eggs well beaten

Salt and pepper to taste. Mix altogether; place in a mold. Set in a pan of water. Steam in hot oven. When firm, turn out and serve with a tomato sauce.

Fried Chicken

Cut chicken in four pieces, put all into a paper bag; add one-half cup flour or more, depending on amount of chicken used. Add salt, and shake vigorously in order to coat all the chicken. In frying pan, melt enough Crisco to cover bottom ½'' deep (it should be very hot) and lay in chicken, skin side first. When that side is crisp, turn and do the other side. Then lower flame and keep turning the pieces until a fork stuck in the middle produces no red juice (about 20 minutes).

When done, remove to a hot platter, scrape up all the bits, add flour to fat, one-half teaspoon dried tarragon (or one teaspoon of fresh) and stir until smooth. Add milk until you reach desired consistency; then season with salt.

Seasoned Hamburgers

Start with one pound of the best grade hamburger meat. Make into six balls, dredge in flour, season with salt and pepper and fry quickly in hot butter (one tablespoon) on both sides. Reduce flame and cook until desired doneness. Remove from frying pan and add to the butter in the pan one-fourth teaspoon dried thyme, one teaspoon onion juice, and one tablespoon Worcestershire sauce. Let cook for a minute, then add two tablespoons brandy, one-fourth cup heavy cream, stirring constantly till thickened. Pour over hamburgers on toast and serve. Garnish with parsley or chervil.

Lulu's Leg of Lamb

1 tsp. marjoram
1 tsp. thyme
1 tsp. rosemary
4 garlic cloves cut in half
1 6-lb. leg of lamb
2 tbsps. olive oil
2 tbsps. flour
1 cup dry white wine
1 tsp. salt, cracked pepper

Mix salt and pepper with olive oil. Spread mixture over entire surface of lamb. Sprinkle with herbs and flour. Make eight little slits in the top of the lamb and insert the garlic halves. Pour wine and one cup of water into bottom of roasting pan. Roast at 325°F. for two-and-a-half hours, basting frequently.

—Marcia Barber

Pork Chops Paysanne

6   pork chops, about 2¼ lbs.
    salt and pepper to taste
1   tbsp. butter
2   cups coarsely chopped onion
1   tsp. finely minced garlic
4   Idaho potatoes, peeled & cubed
4   carrots, peeled & cut into ½-inch lengths
½   cup dry white wine
2   cups water
1   bay leaf
¼   tsp. thyme

Preheat oven to 375°F. Sprinkle chops on both sides with salt and pepper to taste. Melt the butter in a skillet large enough to hold the chops in one layer. Add the chops to the butter and cook about three or four minutes on one side, or until nicely browned. Turn and brown other side. Scatter the onion pieces and garlic around and between the chops. Cook about five more minutes. Scatter the cubed potatoes and carrot pieces around and over the chops. Add the wine, water, bay leaf, thyme, more salt and pepper to taste, and bake, covered, for 45 minutes. Serves six.

Chicken Livers with Rosemary

½ lb. chicken livers
   salt & fresh pepper
1 tbsp. flour
2 tbsp. vegetable oil
1 tbsp. butter
¼ tsp. crushed fresh rosemary leaves
2 tsps. finely chopped shallots
2 tbsps. dry madeira
1 tbsp. finely chopped fresh parsley
   Toast rounds or triangles

Pick over livers and discard any tough membranes. Rinse them well and pat dry. Halve them. Sprinkle the pieces with salt and pepper, and dredge lightly in flour. Heat the oil until it is almost but not quite smoking. Add the livers and cook over high heat, turning as necessary, until golden brown and crisp on the outside, about three minutes. Remove and drain. Wipe out skillet and return to stove, adding butter and, when butter is melted, the livers. Toss quickly, and add rosemary and shallots, and madeira. Bring to a boil quickly, and sprinkle with parsley. Serve on toast rounds or triangles, or on rice. Serves two to four.

Chicken Livers with Port

1 lb. chicken livers
   flour for dredging
   salt & pepper to taste
1 medium onion, chopped
6 pieces bacon
½ cup port, or to taste
1 tsp. thyme
   butter as needed

Fry bacon until crisp; remove to paper towels to drain. Repeat procedure with onions, sauteeing them in the bacon grease until transparent. Wash and dry livers, and dredge them in flour mixed with salt and pepper. Melt butter in skillet, and saute the livers gently until browned and crisp on the outside, but still pink in center. Add bacon, crumbled, and onion, port, and thyme. Cook until seasonings are blended. DO NOT OVERCOOK. Serves four amply.

Above two from Sarah Farwell

Mexican Tongue

Simmer a fresh tongue until tender. Skin and leave in your choice of liquor until cold. Bake in a china or glass dish, basting often until liquid thickens. Serve with raisin sauce.

Sauce: one cup vinegar, one cup sugar, one cup crushed raisins, one lemon, cut in thin slices, two dozen whole cloves.

Cook 20-30 minutes, until well-blended.

Rosemary Chicken

Wash and dry chicken breasts. Place in buttered baking dish. Sprinkle each with one-quarter teaspoon each of rosemary, garlic salt, lemon thyme, and cracked pepper. Dot each breast with butter and a squeeze of lemon juice. Bake at 375°F. for one hour, or barbeque till tender (about one hour). If barbeque method is used, trying using the stems from fresh rosemary to throw into the coals.

—Marcia Barber

Stuffed Round Steak

2½   pounds round steak
     a handful of parsley
2   cloves garlic
½   green pepper
½   tsp. dried thyme

Spread herbs over steak and cover with grated parmesan cheese; slash any rim of fat from meat. Roll meat lengthwise and tie with string in several places. Brown on all sides in butter in casserole dish. Remove to a plate. Fry a few mushrooms in the butter and replace the steak. Add one cup chicken bouillon and one cup Burgundy. Simmer for almost one hour with cover on, basting often. If the sauce has not cooked down enough when the meat is tender, take off the meat and reduce sauce over a high flame. Pour sauce over meat roll and serve very hot.

Vegetables

Baked Rice and Tomato

2 cups plain boiled rice
1 can tomatoes

Stew tomatoes with bay leaf, pinch of basil, a few cloves and an onion. Strain and add one tablespoon butter, one-half tablespoon flour, mixed. Add it to the liquid and pour over the rice. Add a pinch of sugar. Bake slowly for half an hour.

Broccoli Casserole

Cook two packages frozen broccoli. Melt two tablespoons butter in a skillet and fry, but don't brown, a very small onion and one clove of garlic in it. Add two tablespoons flour and enough milk to make a medium-thick white sauce. Add one teaspoon Worcestershire sauce, one tablespoon finely chopped parsley, one teaspoon lemon juice and one-half cup grated parmesan cheese. Blend well, fold in the broccoli, pour into a casserole and top with Pepperidge Farm Herb Seasoned Stuffing, or similar substitute. This adds just the right touch. Bake in the oven for one-half hour at 350°F.

Rissets

Fry one cup uncooked (but washed) rice in one tablespoon butter, and one chopped onion until brown. Remove all to a casserole. Add one cup of chicken stock and cook covered for 20 minutes, adding more stock if necessary. (It should not be wet; it should be the consistency of boiled rice.) Chopped chicken livers may be added. Before serving, stir in one tablespoon parmesan cheese. Stir with fork and serve in casserole.

String Beans with Mushrooms

The quickest and easiest method for this bean dish is to use French-style frozen string beans. Cook them in hot water until tender, drain and arrange in a flat baking dish. Add one teaspoon savory and one-half teaspoon oregano to one can mushroom soup, and pour this over the beans. Sprinkle with grated parmesan cheese and brown in the oven.

Marie's Spinach Border

Cook spinach. Put through grinder or in blender for two seconds or so. Mix with two beaten eggs and one-half cup cream. Put in mold and steam in a pan of water in a moderate oven for at least 30 minutes.

Italian Beans

1	tbsp. oil
3	tbsps. water
1	tbsp. apple cider vinegar
½	tsp. oregano
½	tsp. thyme
1	tbsp. parsley
2-3	cups green beans, cut in 1'' pieces.

In a saucepan combine oil, water and vinegar. Bring to boil. Add herbs and beans cooking slowly for four-six minutes. For four.

Lima Beans with Celery

10	oz. lima beans
1	cup celery, chopped
½	tsp. summer savory
¼	cup beef stock

Bring stock to simmer. Add rest of ingredients and simmer for eight-ten minutes.

Vegetable Stew

4 cups tomatoes, chopped
2 cups carrots, chopped
2 cups celery, chopped
3 cups potatoes, chopped
1 cup endive or dandelion greens, chopped
1 tsp. basil
1 tsp. oregano

Combine ingredients and cook gently about 30 minutes. Serve on brown rice. Serves two-four.

Potatoes and Beans

½   cup stock
2   cups green beans, cut in one-inch pieces
3   potatoes, chopped
1   small onion, chopped
½   tsp. sweet marjoram

In saucepan bring stock to boil. Add beans, potatoes, onion and marjoram. Simmer about fifteen minutes. Serves four-six.

Escalloped Corn

2   cups corn
¼   cup whole wheat flour
2   tbsps. oil
1   tbsp. parsley
¼   tsp. rubbed sage
¾   cup milk

Place corn in one quart baking dish. Stir in flour and oil. Add parsley, sage and milk. Blend well. Bake at 350°F. thirty minutes or until set. Four portions.

Sauté of Broccoli

2 tbsps. oil
1 tbsp. parsley
½ tsp. oregano
1 head broccoli, broken in flowerets

In large skillet heat oil. Mix in herbs. Saute broccoli for several minutes on each side. Serves three-four.

Baked Eggplant

1 eggplant, sliced in ½" rounds
¼ cup butter (½ stick)
¼ cup cheese, grated
4 tomatoes, sliced
1 tsp. basil

Arrange eggplant in oiled baking dish. Melt butter and pour over eggplant, then sprinkle cheese on top. Lay tomatoes on top of cheese and sprinkle with basil. Bake at 375°F. for 35 to 45 minutes. Will serve four.

—Above seven from Bonnie Fisher

Spagetti and Tomato Recipe of an Old Roman Cook

Boil one pound of spaghetti for 10 minutes. Drain dry. Toss into a frying pan of hot oil (one cup) in which chopped onion or one clove of garlic and a few leaves of sweet basil, green or dried, have been previously browned. Turn the spaghetti constantly with two forks, lifting it until the whole is thoroughly saturated with hot oil, salt and pepper. Pour over a tomato sauce made by boiling tomatoes with the herb "bouquet." Serve with grated cheese and a sprinkle of saffron flowers.

"Bouquet" for Tomato Sauce

One small bay leaf, three peppercorns, three cloves (one in each bag), one-half teaspoon thyme, one teaspoon basil, two tablespoons lovage, two tablespoons parsley.

Herbed Green Beans

Steam fresh green beans with one-half minced onion, chopped parsley, one minced garlic clove, one-quarter teaspoon dried basil, one-half teaspoon rosemary. When tender, toss with two tablespoons butter to coat beans. Serve immediately.

Zucchini with Herbs

Wash and slice zucchini one-quarter inch thick. Steam until just tender with one-half medium onion, chopped, one-quarter teaspoon each oregano, sweet basil, marjoram. Sprinkle with one-half cup grated parmesan cheese; toss to coat well and serve immediately.

—Above two recipes from Marcia Barber

The following two sauces have many uses:

Herb Sauce

1   tbsp. butter
1   tbsp. oil
1   tbsp. flour
½   cup milk
½   tsp. dill seeds
½   tsp. celery seeds
1   tbsp. parsley

Heat butter and oil in small pan. Stir in flour to thicken. Slowly blend in milk, stirring until blended and thick. Sprinkle herbs into sauce. Serve over fish or vegetables.

Golden Celery Sauce

½   cup oil
2   tbsps. flour
¾   cup milk
1   cup celery, chopped
2   tbsps. chives, minced
½   tsp. tarragon

Heat oil. Stir in flour until smooth. Slowly stir in milk blending well. Add celery and herbs. Good over broiled fish or baked potatoes.

—Bonnie Fisher

Hot Mushroom Dip

1   cup sour cream
1   lb. sliced mushrooms
4   tbsp. butter
1   clove minced garlic
½ tsp. salt
¼ tsp. pepper
2 tbsps. fresh chopped parsley (include the stems; they contain all the Vitamin C)
½ tsp. chives
½ tsp. chervil

Sauté the mushrooms and garlic in butter. Add seasonings. Remove from flame. Fold in sour cream. Serve in chafing dish; spread on crackers.

Dill Dip

1   cup sour cream
1   cup mayonnaise
2 tbsps. chopped parsley
1   tbsp. chopped dill weed
1   tsp. chopped chives
1   tsp. marjoram

Combine ingredients, chill; serve with fresh raw vegetables.

—Marcia Barber

Mrs. Elizabeth Mackey's Quickies

ONCE A GARDEN CLUB meeting was held in our kitchen during which Elizabeth Mackey gave us a demonstration on how to make "Quickies." She told us that during the hot summer months no one wants to spend long hours in the kitchen and hence she had worked up a series of dishes that could be quickly made, and yet were still tasty. Herbs play an important part in these recipes.

Crab Bisque

1   can crab meat
1   can pea soup
1   can tomato soup
¼   tsp. basil
¼   tsp. summer savory
1   cup milk
½   cup sherry
1   tsp. Worcestershire sauce

Soak crab meat in sherry. Heat other ingredients in double boiler, add crab meat and sherry.

Frozen Peas and Carrot Salad

Cook one package frozen peas and carrots (add one-fourth tsp. marjoram just before they are done). Chill. Add several green onions, finely cut; then add one-fourth cup mayonnaise. Serve on lettuce for buffet, in place of vegetable and/or salad.

Savory Rice

This was a very special mix of Mrs. Mackey's, which can be used as a luncheon dish by adding mushrooms or chicken or tuna fish. You must have a little box of "Savory Rice", which will make many dishes:

Brown two large chopped onions and one cup raw rice (we like the natural brown rice) in three tablespoons butter. Add one tablespoon Savory Rice Mix and three cups bouillon. Cook, stirring occasionally, until liquid is absorbed, about 40 minutes.

Frozen Chopped Spinach Casserole

1 package frozen chopped spinach, thawed
1 package onion soup mix
½ cup sour cream
¼ tsp. marjoram

   Mix, bake until heated

Crab Meat Entree

1 can crab meat or
1 package frozen crab meat
   juice of ½ lemon
¼ tsp. marjoram

   Put all in top of double boiler, heat and serve on toast.

Shrimp DeJonghe

1 can shrimp
¼ cup butter
¼ tsp. salt
1 small clove garlic, crushed
½ tsp. Sea Food mixed herbs, (e.g. basil, tarragon, parsley)
¼ cup sherry or sauterne
3 tbsps. bread crumbs

   Place shrimp in bottom of small casserole. Mix well, spread remaining ingredients over shrimp. Sprinkle with parmesan cheese. Bake in 350°F. oven for 10-15 minutes, until heated through. Place under broiler for one minute. Serves two or three.

Chicken Paprika

1 sliced onion, browned in butter; add 1 teaspoon paprika
4 tbsps. water, simmer until onions are tender
1 can chicken fricassee
½ tsp. tarragon

   Heat thoroughly, but do not boil; add one-fourth cup sour cream (do not mix; just streak into chicken mixture). Serve on rice with shredded almonds on top.

Cheese & Egg Dishes

Egg Timbales

Start with six eggs, slightly beaten. Add a little grated onion, a pinch of salt, twelve shakes of white pepper and a bit of cayenne. Then add one cup milk and a little chopped parsley. Put in a mold and set in a pan of cold water to bake for about 15 minutes in a hot oven. Put paper over them while baking. Serve with Hollandaise or tomato sauce. Serves six.

Herbed Deviled Eggs

Cut hard-boiled eggs in half. Remove and mash yolks. For every two eggs add one tablespoon mayonnaise and one-quarter teaspoon each: celery seed, poppy seed, thyme, oregano and dry mustard. Return mixture to egg white. Garnish with paprika.

—Bonnie Fisher

Eggs Under Glass (Adeline)

Make rounds of toast in little casserole dishes. Drop eggs in a spider of milk and cream, with a little salt. When eggs are cooked, lift them out on the toast. Pour the cream around them. Sprinkle with grated cheese and red pepper. Put the glass on and cook in oven for five minutes.

Eggs au Gratin

Beat the whites of four eggs until they are stiff. Add the beaten yolks, one-half teaspoon salt, a few grains cayenne and mix well. Add one cup grated cheese, one-half cup milk. Pour into individual buttered dishes, one-half full, cover with crumbs, bake for eight minutes in a moderate oven. Serves four.

Cheese Dreams

Sprinkle grated aged cheddar cheese on slices of whole-wheat bread. Sprinkle with summer savory or basil and curry powder. Put under broiler until cheese puffs up (about two minutes). Serve this for luncheon with a salad.

Pinback Cheese Toast

Slice two pieces of bread one-half inch thick. Cut off crusts. Pour over them one egg beaten in milk and seasoned with salt and pepper. Cover the soaked bread with slices of cheese. Bake in a hot oven until the cheese is melted and browned (about 20 minutes). Serve on the platter on which it is cooked. (This can also be cooked in individual baking dishes.)

Tomato Rarebit

Melt two tablespoons butter, blend in two tablespoons of flour and gradually add one-half cup cream. Then add one cup stewed strained tomatoes in which a pinch of soda has been dissolved. Stir until perfectly smooth, and then add one-half teaspoon mustard, one-half teaspoon salt, two cups finely cut, soft American cheese, a dash of cayenne and two eggs slightly beaten.

Serve on toasted crackers as soon as the cheese melts.

Rice Mold

Use a one-quart mold. Put in a layer of cooked rice, then a layer (one-half-inch thick) of parmesan cheese, and so on to the top, using plenty of cheese. Heat in oven to mold and melt the cheese. Serve on a platter with liver sauce around it, or with a tomato sauce.

Liver Sauce

Take two chicken livers, boil them with an onion and a little water, crumbing them with a fork as they cook. Cook until they are a paste (a long time). When they are mashed to a paste, add butter, salt and paprika and one can of tomato sauce. Pour it around the mold.

Cheese Relish

1   cup grated cheese, 1 egg white beaten stiff
1   tsp. curry powder
½   tsp. dried basil
½   tsp. salt
2   dashes of cayenne

Cut bread in small one-half inch rounds. Butter and drop one teaspoon of mixture on each round. Put in oven until just brown; serve immediately. This recipe is enough for six slices. Use aged cheese whenever possible; it has a much better flavor. We use it grated, instead of parmesan.

Cheese and Tomato Luncheon Dish

Make the following cheese sauce and keep hot in a double boiler: Melt two tablespoons butter, add two tablespoons flour and stir in one cup milk. Add salt and pepper and three-fourths cup milk, grated cheese. Stir in well and cook over hot water until cheese is all melted.

In the bottom of a casserole put two onions chopped finely, two sliced tomatoes, sprinkle with two teaspoons chopped parsley, one-fourth teaspoon diced basil. Cover with a cheese sauce and on top of this put three slices of hard-cooked eggs. On top of this put two sliced tomatoes and more parsley and basil. Over all this put more cheese sauce. Bake for 45 minutes in 350°F. oven. Serve at once, in casserole in which it was baked.

Jajij

This is a spread based on cottage cheese, which can be used to stuff celery, tomatoes, or peppers. In its native environment (northern Iran and Turkey) it is used mainly as a summer breakfast spread. It is low in calories and high in protein. Mix together the following ingredients:

1   pint small curd cottage cheese
¼   cup chopped chives, shallots, scallions or a combination
2   tbsps. diced green pepper
1   tsp. fresh or ½ tsp. dry purple basil
1   tsp. chopped coriander
     black pepper to taste.

—Eden Frye

Boo's Best Omelette

5	eggs
1	cup milk
¼	yogurt or sour cream
	dash Tabasco
½	tsp. each of marjoram, thyme, parsley, fennel
2	tsp. chives
2	tsp. butter or margarine
½	cup sliced mushrooms
¼	cup minced onion
½	avocado sliced
½	cup grated Swiss cheese
	alfalfa sprouts

Beat together eggs, milk, yogurt or sour cream, Tabasco, and herbs. Set aside. Sauté onions and mushrooms in butter, remove them from frying pan. Melt two tablespoons butter in omelette pan. Add egg mixture. Cook until almost set. Add onions, mushrooms, sliced avocado and cheese. Fold omelette over and cook until eggs are set and cheese is melted. Garnish with alfalfa sprouts.

Breads, Cakes & Cookies

A GREAT ADDITION TO the food in our household has been an electric flour mill with which we grind the whole wheat berry for making soft, fine, pure flour. This machine stands about three feet high and holds a small hopper on the top into which the wheat berries are poured. In about three minutes a cupful of flour is ground that falls into a small bag at the base of the machine. This flour is so fine that it does not have to be sifted. In this way we know we are getting the full food value from our wheat; nothing is taken out, nothing is added. Result: We have bread, biscuits, cookies, puddings, any dish in which flour is used, with a delicious and unusual flavor. I cannot overemphasize the value of whole wheat flour. If you cannot make your own, buy it from any health food store. A flour mill can be purchased or ordered from any well-stocked health food store. (See the back pages of this book for a directory of health and nature food stores in your area.)

Wherever flour is mentioned in the following recipes, use whole-grain flour, if possible.

Herbed Garlic Bread

Mix one stick of softened butter or margarine with one-quarter teaspoon each of marjoram, thyme and rosemary, and one-half cup grated Parmesan cheese. Spread mixture on each slice of a loaf of French bread. Wrap in foil and heat through.

—*Marcia Barber*

Margaret Dunsire's Bread

3 tbsps. shortening (oleo, butter or bacon drippings; we use the latter)
3 tbsps. honey
1 quart milk
1 tbsp. salt
2 packages dry yeast
6 cups whole- wheat flour

In a small enamel pan on the stove, melt the shortening and honey using low heat. Add the milk and yeast, then the flour and salt. Keep stirring as you add the flour until the dough is stiff enough to knead. Turn out the dough on a floured board and knead for about eight minutes. Put in a large well-greased bowl, and leave to rise until double its size. Turn out on floured board again, give it a few more punches, divide it into three loaves; put in greased loaf pans, let rise again until double in size, then bake in a 375°F. oven for about 50 minutes.

Margaret Dunsire's Nut Bread

2¼ cups of whole-wheat flour
2½ tsps. baking powder
1   tsp. baking soda
¾   tsp. salt
¾   cup brown sugar
1   cup nuts, ground

Mix above ingredients together, stir in one-and-one-half cups of sour milk or buttermilk. (To make sour milk, put one-and-one-half tablespoons vinegar in one-and-one-half cups milk.) Stir well and place in a well greased eight inch by four inch bread pan. Bake in a moderately hot oven (350°F.) for about one-and-one-half hours.

Margaret Dunsire's Scotch Shortbread

4 cups sifted flour
1 cup sugar
1 lb. butter

Cream the butter and sugar. Add flour very slowly, creaming well. Pat it out flat on a flour board. Divide into parts for cookies or cakes. Put onto a buttered tin, prick the dough with a fork. Bake in 275°F. oven for 30 minutes, or until done.

Nut Bread

2   cups white flour
2   cups graham or whole-wheat flour
1   egg
1   tsp. salt
1   cup English walnuts, chopped
1½ cups milk
4   tsps. baking powder
1   cup molasses

Sift the two flours into a bowl, add the salt, nuts, baking powder. Beat the egg, mixing with the molasses and milk. Mix all together and turn into a buttered bread tin or baking dish. Allow to rise for twenty minutes, then put in oven to bake slowly for an hour at 300°F. or perhaps a bit less.

Adeline's Corn Cake

4 tbsps. corn meal
1 tbsps. white flour
1 tsp. salt
2 tbsps. sugar
3 tbsps. melted butter

Melt the butter. Combine the dry ingredients. Pour about one-half cup boiling water over the mixture to make it soft. Combine with the melted butter and mix well. Drop from a spoon or a buttered sheet, and bake in a medium-hot (350°F.) oven 10-12 minutes. Do not drop too thickly.

Maggie's Rhode Island Corn Cakes

2 cups boiling water
1 cup corn meal

Stir one tablespoon butter, one-half teaspoon sugar and one-half teaspoon salt into the water. Add corn meal. Spread very thin with a spatula on a buttered pan (about one inch thick). Cover thinly with cream and bake for one-half hour. Allow to cool before serving, then heat again (otherwise it will be soggy). This is good to eat with syrup, like pancakes.

Spoon Bread

1   egg, beaten
¾   cup corn meal
1½ cups buttermilk
½   tsp. baking soda
½   tsp. summer savory

Stir ingredients together with wire whisk. Bake in oiled 9" pan for 20-25 minutes at 400°F. or until set in center.

—Bonnie Fisher

Mrs. George Cobb's Beaten Biscuits

2   cups pastry flour
1   tbsp. lard
1   tsp. salt
½ cup milk
½ cup water

Melt the lard and add to the remaining ingredients. Mix all to a good consistency, then put through a meat chopper (or, once again, a food processor). Put it through until light. Roll out, cut with a biscuit cutter. Mark through with a fork, and bake in a moderate oven for 15 or 20 minutes.

Adeline's Sponge Cake

6 eggs (separated) weighed with equal amount of sugar
½ the weight of eggs in flour
    juice of half a lemon

Beat the yolks and sugar together with the lemon juice; continue to beat very lightly. Beat the whites stiff, and fold into the beaten yolks. Sift the flour and cut into beaten eggs. Pour into buttered cake pans in spoonfuls. Bake 15 minutes in medium-hot oven. Sift a little powdered sugar on top of each cake.

Mrs. Cotting's Gems

4 cups high-quality white flour
2 cups warm water
1 cup milk

Place gem pans on stove. Get them very hot and well buttered. Pour mixture into blender and beat all ingredients thoroughly for at least one minute. Pour into gem pans and bake in hot oven 20-25 minutes. Serve immediately.

Snipidoodles

This is a good cake to make when eggs are expensive or scarce:

1   cup sugar
1   cup flour
½   cup milk
1   egg
1   tsp. baking powder in the flour
1   tbsp. butter

Cream the butter and sugar together; gradually add the egg (well beaten), the milk and flour, spread in thin sheets in baking tin, cook in moderate oven until done (about half an hour). Sprinkle with sugar in which one-half teaspoon cinnamon has been mixed.

Ethel's Hermits

1½ cups dark brown sugar
⅔   cup butter
2   eggs
2   tbsps. milk
1   tsp. cinnamon
1   tsp. nutmeg
1   tsp. cloves
1   tsp. baking soda
1   cup chopped raisins
     Flour as needed

Put all ingredients together in a bowl; add enough flour so mixture can be rolled. Put in greased pan and cut in squares when cooked, before it hardens. (Use moderate-hot oven.)

Maggie's Oatmeal Crisps

Take cooked oatmeal and spread thinly over a buttered pan. Pour cream over this and bake for 20 minutes.

Margarets

1   cup brown sugar
2   eggs
½   cup flour
¼   tsp. baking powder
1   cup chopped pecans

Beat eggs; add sugar, flour (into which baking powder has been added) and pecans. Bake in well-greased tins, putting a nut meat on top when cooked.

Chocolate Brownies

½   cup butter
1   cup sugar
2   eggs, beaten 'til light
½   cup flour
2   squares chocolate, melted
½   cup English Walnuts, chopped fine

Cream butter, add sugar gradually, then add eggs. Then add flour, melted chocolate and, finally, the walnuts. Put in a greased pan and bake 10-15 minutes in a moderate-hot oven (350°F.). Let cool, cut in strips. Makes two pans.

Coconut Muffins

2   eggs beaten
2   tbsps. honey
1   cup milk
1½ cups whole wheat flour
1   tbsp. orange peel
½   cup coconut

Stir honey into beaten eggs. Blend in milk. Add flour and blend well. Stir in orange peel and coconut. Fill oiled muffin pans about three-quarters full. Bake at 350°F. 25-30 minutes.

—Bonnie Fisher

Gossamer Gingerbread

½ cup butter
½ cup sugar
½ cup milk
1¼ cups whole-grain flour
1 tsp. ginger

Have tin sheets well-cooled, and rub with shortening. Mix all ingredients, then spread thinly on the tin with a knife (as thinly as possible). Bake in a hot (but not overheated, about 375°F.-400°F.) oven. Cut and remove from sheet before it cools.

Ping-Pong Cookies

1 tbsp. butter
1 cup sugar
2 eggs
2 tsps. baking powder
2 tsps. vanilla
2 cups rolled oats

Cream butter and sugar; add the eggs, well beaten. Then add other ingredients. Drop with a spoon on a cookie sheet, and bake 10 minutes in moderate oven.

Lizzie Driscoll's Almond Wafers

½ cup butter
1 cup sugar
½ cup milk
1 cup flour
½ cup almonds, chopped fine or grated

Cream butter and sugar. Add milk, drop by drop, being careful that it does not curdle. Then add flour and spread on buttered sheets with a broad-bladed knife, as thin as possible. Shake a generous amount of almonds on each sheet before putting it in the oven. Bake in a very slow oven (about 250°F.) for about 15 minutes. When done, cut in squares while hot.

Sarah von Dael's Cookies

½ cup butter or margarine
½ cup white sugar
½ cup brown sugar
1 egg
1 tsp. vanilla

Sift together:
1 cup whole-grain flour
½ tsp. salt
½ tsp. baking powder
½ tsp. soda
1 cup quick oatmeal
½ cup nut meats, chopped

Cream sugar with butter; beat in egg, add vanilla. Add this to the sifted dry ingredients. Mix well and drop by spoon on greased cookie sheet. Press down with fork. Cook about 15 minutes in 375°F. oven.

Brown Cake

2 eggs
¼ cup butter, melted
¾ cup molasses
½ cup yogurt
2 cups buckwheat flour
1 tsp. cinnamon
2 tsps. baking soda

Beat eggs till foamy. Stir in butter, molasses and yogurt. Add dry ingredients and beat fifty times. Pour into two greased cake pans. Bake at 375°F. for 30-40 minutes.

—*Bonnie Fisher*

Desserts & Sweets

The uses of honey

HONEY WAS THE SOLE source of sweetening in the old days, and how unfortunate it is for our health and well-being that today so few people know how to use it in place of refined sugar. As a natural sweet, honey is wholesome and contains many minerals that are lacking in our refined white sugar.

Honey contains iron, copper, sodium potassium, manganese, calcium, magnesium and phosphorus, which are all essential to the good nutrition of animals. These minerals are present in honey, although in some cases only in trace quantities. Honey's varying flavors depend on the kinds of flowers from which the bees take pollen. An herb garden near your bee hive will give you unusual and delicate tasting honey the like of which is almost impossible to buy. In the old herbals we read of honey being eaten to help ward off cancer, and of the sting of a bee helping those suffering from arthritis and rheumatism. In our family we have had remarkable cures by taking bee sting pills for bursitis shoulders. These pills can be obtained from various druggists, in addition to a variety of other sources.

Honey will keep indefinitely and does not have to be kept refrigerated. It is best not to have it in direct sunlight, and to avoid damp places for storage since it absorbs and retains moisture.

In using honey for cooking, reduce the amount of liquid by one-quarter for each cup of honey used to replace sugar. Be sure to remember its many uses.

Eat honey for breakfast, with your toast. Use it in desserts wherever possible; experiment with it, and you may prefer it to any other form of sweetening. Use it directly from the comb or unheated, so as to get its full nutritional value.

When measuring honey, molasses, or corn syrups, it helps to oil the measuring cup or spoon first. This way, the honey will not stick to the sides.

Honey Sauce

1 cup honey
1 cup cream
1 tbsp. mint

Whip the cream and add the honey slowly, whipping until throughly mixed. It should be very stiff when served. Place in bowl or glass pitcher from which it is to be served, and place in icebox to chill for several hours. Just before serving, sprinkle mint over top. This is delicious to use on fruits or puddings, and should be ladled out with a spoon.

Honey Custard

3   eggs
⅓   cup honey
4   cups scalded milk
⅛   tsp. cinnamon
     a pinch salt and grated chocolate

Beat the eggs enough to homogenize the yolks and whites, but not so much that you make them foamy. Add the other ingredients. Bake in cups or in a large pan in a moderate-heat oven. The baking dishes should be set in water as they bake, in the traditional custard-baking method. Then cool, sprinkle with grated chocolate and serve with cream.

Honey Charlotte Russe

1   quart cream
1   package lady fingers (or similar thin cakes)
½   cup honey
1   package gelatine
2   tbsps. rum or kirsch

Whip the cream and add the honey, mixing the two well together. Then add the dissolved gelatine and liqueur. Line a mold with ladyfingers and fill it with the mixture. Serve very cold.

Honey Mousse

4 eggs
1 pint cream
1 cup honey
1 package gelatine

Beat the eggs slightly and slowly pour the honey over them. Put this in a double boiler, and cook very slowly until the mixture thickens. When it is cool, add the dissolved gelatine and the cream, whipped. Put the mixture into a mold and place in the refrigerator. Serve cold.

Chocolate Peppermint Parfait

Start with eight or ten thin chocolate-covered mints. Put them in the top of a double boiler to melt. Cook two-thirds cup sugar and one-fourth cup water until it spins a thread. Pour this slowly over the stiffly beaten whites of two eggs, and beat constantly until very thick and fluffy. Add one-half cup heavy cream and one teaspoon vanilla to the melted peppermints, and mix well; then add this to the beaten mixture. Fold in one cup of stiffly beaten cream and pour into freezing tray. Like all parfaits, this should never be frozen hard, but only to a very thick mush. Serve in tall parfait glasses.

Creme Brulée

Pour one cup of heavy cream in the top of a double boiler and bring it to a boil. Beat two eggs and one-half pound brown sugar together until smooth, and add to cream. Cook for five minutes, beating constantly until it is thick like custard. Pour into glass dish and let stand for two hours, without moving. Sprinkle heavily with brown sugar and put under the broiler until the sugar melts and just begins to harden. This is the only tricky bit, it must be watched constantly, for if it gets too hard it will shatter when served. Set in refrigerator for at least three hours so it may be served very cold.

Pot-de-Creme Chocolat

Take two large milk chocolate bars (four-and-a-half ounce size). Break them up and put on top of double boiler with one square bitter chocolate and eight tablespoons water. When the chocolate is all melted, remove from the fire and stir in four egg yolks. Stir the mixture until very smooth. Cool and fold in four stiffly beaten egg whites. Pour into glasses or custard cups and let stand in the refrigerator for at least three hours. Serves six people.

Biscuit Tortoni

1	cup whipped cream
1	cup powdered sugar
1	egg white
½	cup macaroon crumbs
3	tbsps. sherry
1	pinch salt

Gradually add the sugar to the whipped cream, then fold in stiffly-beaten egg white, and all but one tablespoon of macaroon crumbs. Add sherry and salt and pack in fluted paper cups. Sprinkle tops with macaroon crumbs and set in refrigerator to freeze. A dozen portions serves six.

Maple Parfait

1	egg yolk
1	cup maple syrup
1	pinch salt
½	pint heavy cream
1	tbsp. gelatin (dissolved)

Beat the yolks until light. Add maple syrup and cook, stirring constantly till thick enough to coat the spoon. Turn into a bowl and beat until cold. Whip the cream and fold in the maple mixture and gelatin. Serve with a sauce of hot maple syrup to which crumbled pecan nuts have been added. Serves six.

Cheese Mold with Fruit

1 lb. cottage cheese
1 large package cream cheese
1 cup heavy cream
1 qt. fruit (strawberries, raspberries, cherries, or peaches)
1 tbsp. gelatine

Rub the cheese through a sieve, add cream and mix well. Mix gelatine in one cup cold water, then melt it over hot water and add to cheese and cream, stirring it well. Pour into circular mold. When set, turn out on to a platter and fill the center with fruit. Serves eight.

Theresa's Rice Pudding

3 eggs separated
2 tbsps. sugar

Beat yolks and add sugar. Boil one cup of rice in one quart of milk. After rice is cool add it and the milk to sugar and eggs. Have rice thick. Add a little vanilla and fold in the whites of eggs, beaten stiff. Bake for one-half hour at 350°F.

Molasses Cookies

¼ cup honey
1 egg
½ cup Blackstrap molasses
⅓ cup butter, melted
2 tbsps. oil
1 tsp. nutmeg
3 cups whole wheat flour

Cream honey and egg. Stir in molasses, butter and oil. Add dry ingredients and blend completely. Form dough into three balls. On a floured surface roll out dough to about one-quarter inch thickness. Cut out round shapes. Bake at 375°F. for 8-10 minutes. Makes about eight dozen one-and-one-half inch round cutouts.

Apple Chew

6   cups apples, sliced
1   cup whole wheat flour
1   cup oatmeal
½   cup sunflower seeds
½   teaspoon dill seeds
⅓   cup butter, softened
½   cup honey

Place sliced apples in shallow baking dish. Mix together flour, oatmeal, seeds, butter and honey. Sprinkle topping on apples. Bake at 375°F. for 30-40 minutes.

Banana-Walnut Cake

2½ cups whole wheat flour
1   tsp. baking powder
1   tsp. baking soda
½   tsp. mace
½   cup honey
⅔   cup oil
⅔   cup buttermilk
1⅓ cups ripe mashed bananas
2   eggs
⅔   cup walnuts, chopped

Blend flour, baking powder, soda and mace. Add honey, oil, one-third cup buttermilk and bananas. Beat well. Add eggs and remaining buttermilk. Mix well. Fold in nuts. Pour into two nine inch pans and bake at 350°F. about thirty five minutes.

Orange Coffee Cake

¼   cup oil
⅓   cup honey
1   egg
½   cup orange juice
1½ cups whole wheat flour
2   tsps. baking powder
1   small orange, cut in wedges
1   tbsp. orange peel

Cream oil, honey and egg. Stir in juice. Mix in flour and baking powder. Spread batter in greased nine by nine inch pan. Press in orange wedges and sprinkle with orange peel. Bake thirty minutes at 375°F.

—Above four from Bonnie Fisher

Mrs. Hill's Plum Pudding

3 pints milk
6 crackers pounded fine
5 eggs
1 small cup currants
1 cup sugar
1 tbsp. molasses
1 ground nutmeg
1 tsp. cinnamon
1 tsp. salt
   Butter, size of an egg
1 glass red wine

Cream the butter and sugar. Mix the dry ingredients together and then add to wet ingredients. Mix all well together and bake in a buttered baking dish. Serve with hard sauce.

Aunt Abby's Indian Pudding [*either hot or cold*]

Add to one quart boiled milk one cup Indian meal, and boil in double boiler for 10 minutes. Then add one cup molasses, one cup of milk, one cup of water, one-half cup sugar, one tablespoon butter, one teaspoon salt, one tablespoon ginger. Let this mixture cool, then add two well-beaten eggs. Bake in a deep buttered dish for two or three hours in a slow oven.

Gingerbread Apple Pudding

6   apples
½   cup sugar
½   tsp. powdered cinnamon
1   cup molasses
½   cup boiling water
1   tsp. baking soda
½   tsp. powdered ginger
     pinch of salt

Peel and slice the apples, then add sugar, salt and cinnamon and place in a buttered baking dish. Melt the butter, add it to the molasses with the ginger, and add the soda (dissolved in a very littl boiling water.) Add enough flour to make a thin batter. Pour this mixture over the apples and bake in a moderate oven for half an hour. Serve with whipped or plain cream.

Francatelli

Pour one pint boiling milk on ten tablespoons of fine bread crumbs, let soak 10 minutes. Add the yolks of four eggs, well beaten, add six tablespoons melted butter and a pinch of salt. Flavor with lemon or vanilla. Finally, stir in whites of four eggs, beaten stiff, and bake quickly (400°F.) in a buttered baking dish.

Dandy Pudding

1   pint milk
3   eggs
½   cup sugar
2   tbsps. corn starch
1   pinch salt

Scald the milk and stir in the corn starch, mixed with one-half cup cold milk. Salt and stir until it thickens. Add the yolks of the eggs, beaten to a cream, with the sugar. Cook 10 minutes, stirring well, and turn in to a shallow glass baking dish. Peel eight peaches, steam them until tender, and when cold lay them over the pudding. Frost with the whites of three eggs and put in a quick oven. Brown lightly and serve cold.

Coconut Pudding

Boil one quart milk, a little butter, with salt added. Put one grated coconut in the hot milk. Add three-quarter cup sugar and four eggs, well beaten. Mix all together and bake one-half hour.

Snow Balls

Beat the yolks of three eggs until thick. Add one-and-one-half cups sugar, one-half cup cold water, one teaspoon lemon juice, two cups of flour, two teaspoons baking powder. Fold in the whites of three eggs, beaten stiff, and pour into buttered earthen cups. Steam 30 minutes. Cover with powdered sugar and serve with cream or creamy sauce.

Frosted Apples

Peel apples and stew in thin syrup until they become tender, but be careful they don't break. Then dip these in the white of an egg that has been whipped to a stiff froth, and sift powdered sugar over them quickly. Put in oven a few minutes, then serve.

Grandma Hill's Mincemeat

4   pint bowls of chopped meat (about 12 lbs.)
6   pint bowls chopped apple
1   lb. suet
2½ lbs. beef drippings and butter, ½ of each
3   bowls sugar
2   bowls stoned raisins
1   bowl currants
1   teacupful chopped citron
1   pint molasses
1   pint sherry
1. pint whiskey
1   pint cider (old-fashioned pints)
½   teacupful salt
½   teacupful cinnamon
½   teacupful clove
3   nutmegs

Mix and cook thoroughly for two hours. If not soft enough, add some of the liquid the meat was cooked in. Store in a large crock and use for mince pies as needed.

Marshmallow Pudding

Get one-half pound marshmallows and cut each one in four pieces with scissors. Soak overnight in the refrigerator in three-quarters cup sherry. Whip one pint heavy cream and add one-half cup confectioners sugar; fold in marshmallows, decorate with candied mint leaves and maraschino cherries and leave in cold refrigerator until needed. This may be doubled or halved with equally good results. As given, it serves 10.

Henrietta's Prune Pudding

Soak one pound prunes overnight in enough water to cover them. The next morning add one-half cup coffee, one-half cup sugar. Stew until soft, stone and cut in one inch pieces. Beat the whites of three eggs stiff enough to stand; gradually add one-half cup sugar to this. Add the prunes, mix well, set on ice. Serve with cream.

Minted Fresh Pears

Steam fresh pears and two tablespoons fresh (or two teaspoons dried) mint leaves just until tender. Melt butter or margarine in saucepan. Add pears and mint and reheat.

—Marcia Barber

Peach Foam

Pare and cut six large peaches in halves; rub them through a sieve and sweeten with one-half cup powdered sugar. Beat whites of three eggs and add to sweetened pulp until thick and smooth. Turn into mold, chill on ice and serve with whipped cream.

Aunt Sue's Usuals

Take two cups Indian meal; pour in enough boiling water to make this a thick batter. Add two well-beaten eggs, one-half cup milk, one-quarter teaspoon soda and one-half cup well-sifted flour. Form into balls and drop into hot fat from a tablespoon. Serves 8-10 people.

Lizzie Edwards' Chocolate Pie

2   eggs
½   cup butter
1   cup sugar
2   cups whole grain flour
3   tsps. Royal baking powder
⅔   cup milk

Cake: Cream shortening, add sugar slowly. Beat well, adding eggs one at a time. Add sifted dry ingredients alternately with milk. Divide in halves. Bake in greased layer pan at 375°F. for 25 minutes.

Frosting for Pie

¾ cup powdered sugar
2 squares bitter chocolate
2 eggs
2 cups cream

Melt chocolate on top of double boiler in three tablespoons cream; then add sugar. When dissolved, add the eggs, well-beaten, to the chocolate mixture. Beat the two cups cream and fold into the chocolate mixture. Spread between the two cakes and all over the top. This will make enough frosting for one pie.

Strawberries à la Créme

1 qt. berries, soaked in 3 tbsps. Port
1 cup whipping cream
2 tbsps. confectioners' sugar

Whip the cream, add sugar and fold in the berries. Pile in your best kitchen bowl and set in refrigerator for an hour before serving. Serves six.

Simple Dessert with Fresh, Canned or Frozen Fruits

1 cup fruit
6 large marshmallows
1 cup cream
1 tsp. vanilla

Place all ingredients in liquid blender, run the blender for about one minute. Put in bowl or individual dishes and leave in icebox for two-three hours before serving, or until well chilled. Then sprinkle a little dried mint over the top.

Blueberry Pudding

Butter slices of bread and remove crusts. Line a mold with these slices. Stew a quart of blueberries, sweetened to taste, or use canned blueberries, and pour these into the mold. Add another layer of bread and more blueberries until mold is filled. Set in icebox overnight. Turn out on a platter and serve with cream.

Maple Custard

Beat two eggs until a spoonful can be lifted without stringing. Add one-fourth cup maple syrup, one-fourth teaspoon salt, stir well, then add one-and-one-half cups milk. Wet the inside of mold or individual cups with cold water. Strain mixture into the mold or cups. The hot water in the pan, in which the custards are set to bake, should not boil after baking is begun. Bake 45 minutes at 350°F. or until custard is set.

Watermelon Surprise

Cut a small watermelon in half, lengthwise, and remove its pulp with a melon cutter. Mix this with cantaloupe balls, cherries, pitted grapes, and any other fruit you like. Marinate all day in one cup sherry, to which three tablespoons chopped mint and one tablespoon chopped lemon balm have been added. Before serving return to chilled watermelon shell. Decorate with sprigs of mint dipped in whites of egg and dusted with granulated sugar, to give a frosted look.

Ginger Cream

Soak one envelope of gelatine in one-quarter cup of cold water. Heat one quart of milk and add the beaten yolks of four eggs. Add one-half cup sugar and pinch of salt. Cook until it thickens, then add the soaked gelatine. Strain into a pan, add one-and-one-half tablespoons brandy, three teaspoons ginger and one-quarter pound ginger cut in small pieces. When thick, add one pint whipped cream. Turn all into a mold and put in icebox.

Tapioca Cream Pudding

Soak three tablespoons pearl tapioca in cold water until soft. Put pint of milk in double boiler and scald. When hot, add tapioca, one-half cup sugar, pinch of salt and the yolks of two eggs, beaten. Cook until thick, then pour into serving dish and flavor with vanilla. When partly cool, fold in the stiffly beaten whites of the eggs or heap them on the top. Serve with cream.

Tea Cream

1   box gelatine, soaked in a cup of milk for one hour
1   large cup of tea, poured on the dissolved gelatine
½   cup sugar

Let it stiffen, and when it is thick add the whites of two eggs, well-beaten, and a cup of heavy cream. Beat all well and put in a mould or individual cups.

Meringue au Chocolat

Beat three egg whites until nearly stiff, then add one-quarter teaspoon cream of tartar and three-quarters cup sugar, one tablespoon at a time, and beat until very stiff. Put in a Pyrex pie plate, building it up a little on the sides so it will hold a filling when done. Bake for one hour at 250°F. When done, remove from oven and cool. Melt two packages (six ounces each) of semi-sweet chocolate bits over hot water. Add one-quarter cup boiling water and one tablespoon instant coffee. Beat like fudge until creamy and cool. Then add one teaspoon vanilla and fold in the white of another egg, beating until very stiff. Just before serving, put filling into shell and top with one cup whipped cream, into which you should put two tablespoons confectioners sugar and two tablespoons rum or brandy.

Panocha

2   cups brown sugar
½   cup milk

Stir constantly while boiling, until it sugars at the edge, then add small cup chopped English walnuts. Pour onto buttered papers and mark off while warm.

Molasses Candy

1 cup molasses
2 cups sugar
1 tbsp. vanilla

Boil 10 minutes, and pull when cool enough.

Mrs. Elton Clarks' Fudge

2½   cups sugar
¾   cup milk
4   squares bitter chocolate
      butter, size of an egg; pinch of salt

Boil first three ingredients until it sugars around the edge of pan. Add vanilla and butter. Beat hard and pour into buttered pan. This will make one medium-sized panful, equal to one pound.

Margaret Blaney's Fudge

1   lb. powdered sugar
¼   lb. unsweetened chocolate
2   butter balls
1   cup cream

Stir cream and sugar together until it begins to boil. Then add chocolate, boil about two minutes, or until done. Add butterballs and two tablespoons vanilla and beat hard. Pour in buttered tin.

Candy (Made without cooking)

1   cup raisins
1   cup figs
1   cup dates, seeded
1   cup walnuts or pecans
½   cup honey
    Sesame seeds

Grind the first four ingredients in a meat grinder or processor. Place all this in a bowl and mix with honey. Put in a small pan, spread out flat, leave in the icebox a few hours. Cut into squares and roll in the sesame seeds.

Herb & Aromatic teas

LITTLE IS KNOWN OF herb teas (tisanes, as the French call them). In France, to this day, an herb tea is served to guests just before retiring in order to help digestion and aid sleep. Herb teas give us our vitamins as we were meant to have them, instead of in synthetic doses, in pills. If you have not explored the possibilities of herbs and flowers in your garden for making clear, amber-colored and fragrant teas, you have missed a great opportunity.

Aromatic teas may be made from dry or fresh herb flowers, leaves, seeds or roots. If the green leaves are used, allow one handful to the cup. For dried herbs, one or two teaspoons will be sufficient for each cup of boiling water.

How to prepare them:

Place herbs in a china, glass, or graniteware tea pot (never a metal one). Pour over them water that has been boiling for three minutes, and allow it to steep for 10 minutes. Strain this into a cup and flavor with honey and lemon, never cream and sugar. Cold beverages are made in the same way; just let the drink cool and add ice cubes before serving.

Mint Tea (*as made in Morocco*)

1 tsp. green tea per person
1 tsp. sugar per person, or 1 tsp. honey
One handful mint.

Pour boiling water over the mixture. Let steep three minutes. Strain and serve in glasses.

Lemon Balm Tea, Hot

2 tsp. honey
12 sprigs fresh lemon balm or 6 tsp. dried lemon balm
6 cloves

Put lemon balm, honey and cloves into china teapot. Pour one pint boiling water over them. Leave to steep for about 10 minutes, covered. Strain and serve. Makes two cups.

Rose Hip Tea

2 tsp. rose hips
6 cloves
2 tsp. honey
6 tsp. dried balm

Put all ingredients together in china teapot. Pour one pint boiling water over all and let steep 10 minutes. Strain and serve. (Rose hips are very high in vitamin C.)

Peppermint Tea

1 tsp. dried peppermint
1 tsp. honey
1 cup boiling water

Place peppermint and honey in a china teapot. Pour over the boiling water. Allow to steep for 10 minutes; strain, and serve. This can be made without the honey if you do not care to have it so sweet. If taken before retiring, it is conducive to sleep.

Lemon Balm Punch

Start with two big handfuls fresh lemon balm leaves. Then in an enamel pot pour two quarts boiling water over this and allow to steep for 20 minutes. Strain. Add two tablespoons honey, cool. Just before serving add ice and one quart ginger ale. Float bits of mint on top. These proportions can be changed according to taste. Some like more ginger ale and honey. Serves about 15.

Variegated peppermint (above left) and lemon thyme, two favorite sources for herbal teas. Used dry or fresh, they provide a good aroma, soothing taste. Sweeten with honey or maple syrup instead of refined sugar. Photo by Hollis Keats

12

Encyclopedia of herbs

A condensed listing of the most common 300 herbs used in North America, with current Hortus Third *Latin root-name origins. Includes descriptions of uses and characteristics of each herb, with suggestions on how to grow them.*

Explanation of symbols used:

USES:

C — Culinary
M — Medicinal
I — Inspect repelling
H — Household
D — Dye plant

SOWING TIME:

1. Early spring
2. Late spring
3. Late summer or early fall
4. Late fall or early winter

A—annual B—biennial P—perennial h—hardy t—tender

Sample listing: COMMON NAME (S); (Botanical Name-Hortus Third); [Former bot. name, if different], uses, characteristics, height, individual requirements and description.

USES	NAME	SOWING TIME
M	**ACONITE, MONKSHOOD;** (*Aconitum Napellus*) PH, 4'. Blue flowers, requires shade; used for external linaments. Requires cold spell before germinating. Poisonous.	1,4
M,I	**ADONIS, PHEASANT'S EYE;** (*Adonis Aestivalis*) A, 1'. Light, sandy soil. Brilliant red flowers; for kidney, heart disorders; root non-toxic insecticide.	1,4
M,D	**AGRIMONY;** (*Agrimonia Eupatoria*) hP, 3-4'. Astringent, tonic, diuretic, for liver complaints, gall stones, blood diseases. Also used for yellow dye.	1,4
D	**ALKANET;** (*Anchusa Officinalis*) [Alkana tinctora] P, 24-30''. Sow seeds in flats in March, ordinary well-drained garden soil, sun. Roots for red dye.	2
C,M	**ALLSPICE;** (*Pimenta Dioica*) Tree to 30', tropical evergreen. Spice, condiment, aromatic, stimulant and carminative to digestive system. Min. winter temp. 55°F. Grow in large tubs or pots using loam, leafmold and sand.	
M,C	**AMARANTHUS HYPOCONDRIACUS;** (*A. Hybridus 'erythrostachus'*) A, 4'. Red or purplish flowers, astringent; young leaves for pot herb, seeds nutritious meal or flour.	2
C,M	**ANGELICA;** (*Angelica Archangelica*) hP, 6'. Moist, medium rich, cool spot, part shade. Large umbels of greenish white flowers. Easily grown; aromatic, diuretic, for colic, heartburn. Do not cover seed after sowing.	1,4
C,M,I	**ANISE;** (*Pimpinella anisum*) A, 18''. Seeds used as condiment, carminative, for coughs, catarrh. Oil of Anise used against insects.	1,2
M,C	**ANISE HYSSOP;** (*Agastache Foeniculum*) hP, 4'. Fragrant, anise scented, nice tea plant, excellent bee plant, dense spikes of lavender blue flowers June to frost. Prefers some shade.	3,1

M   **ARNICA;** (*Arnica Montana*) P. Leaves form a flat   1,2
rosette, orange-yellow flowers on tall stalk. Loam,
peat and sand. For EXTERNAL use to promote
healing of wounds, bruises, chapped lips, cold sores;
foot bath; to aid hair growth.

C,M,I   *BASILS:*   2
Light soil, medium rich, moist, warm location. Start
indoors early spring for early crop. May be potted
for winter use indoors. For tomato dishes, pea soup,
salads, cheese, poultry dressing. Said to clear brain
and disperse headache. Will discourage flies.

SWEET BASIL; (*Ocimum basilicum*) A, 2'.

SWEET FINE BASIL; (*O. Basilicum*) A. Lower
growing, compact, with numerous finer, smaller
leaves.

LETTUCE LEAF BASIL; (*O. Basilicum crispum*)
A. Larger leaves makes this one best for drying.

LEMON BASIL; (*O. citriodorum*) A, from
Thailand, a neat bushy little plant, more branched
and having smaller leaves than sweet basil, with an
intense, delightful lemon fragrance. Excellent for
teas, potpourri.

DARK OPAL BASIL; (*O. Basilicum 'pur-
purascens'*) A. Deep purplish foliage, pink flowers,
very ornamental, nice border plant, as well as for
seasoning. Turns white vinegar a bright ruby.

SACRED BASIL; (*O. Sanctum*) tP, 2'. More stiffly
erect. Grown in gardens and near temples, considered by the Hindus as a most sacred plant.

AFRICAN BASIL; (*O. Canum*) [O. Kiliman-
descharicum] tP, 3'. Taller, stiffly erect branches,
white flowers, camphor scented, from Kenya, used
for colds and fevers.

C,M,I   **BAY;** (*Laurus Nobilis*) tP. Large shrub or small tree.   3,1
Shiny, dark green leaves, very attractive, fragrant
leaves for soups, stews; keeps insects out of flour

bins. Slow germinating; soak seed, may take from three months up to two years.

M,D,H **BEDSTRAW**; (*Galium verum*) hP, 1-3''. Delicate foliage bright green, good ground cover, sun or part shade. Used to curdle milk in cheese making. Medicinally a refrigerant, diuretic. Tops, yellow dye; roots, red dye. Fragrant yellow flowers throughout summer.   2,3

M **BELLADONNA**; (*Atropa Belladonna*) hP, 3'. Source of Atropine, narcotic, anti-spasmodic, relaxant. Flowers dark purple, shining black berries. Leaves gathered while plant in flower. Eye diseases. POISONOUS.   4

M **BERGAMOT, WILD**; (*Monarda fistulosa*) [Monarda punctata] hP, 2'. Medicinal, aromatic teas, lavender flowers.   1,3

M **BETONY, WOOLY**; (*Stachys Byzantina*) [Stachys lantana] hP. Soft, densely white wooly leaves, small bright purple flowers 12-18'' high, very attractive to bees. Grown for decorative foliage, to facilitate healing on cuts and ulcers.   1,3

M **BETONY**; (*Stachys officinalis*) P, 3'. Dense spike of red-purple flowers. Whole herbs used as nervine, tonic, for headache, neuralgia. Full sun.   1,2

M **BLAC COHOSH**; (*Cimicifuga racemosa*) hP, 3'. Moist, shady location. Astringent, alternative, antidote against poisons and snakebite. Used in whooping-cough, infantile disorders and rheumatism.   1,2

M **BLESSED THISTLE**; (*Cnicus benedictus*) [Carduus benedictus] 1. Spiny-leaved, vigorous, very striking in flower and foliage. Increases milk for nursing mothers.   1,2

BLUE CURLS, CAMPHOR WEED; (*Trichostema Lanceolatum*) hP, 3-6''. Likes dry area, attractive blue flowers, strongly scented, good bee plant. Used by Indians to stupefy fish.   1,3

M **BONESET;** (*Eupatorium perfoliatum*) hP, 2-4'. 1,2
Large, white flower heads, slightly aromatic. Tonic,
diaphoretic, for muscular rheumatism, cold, influenza. Likes ample moisture.

C,M **BORAGE;** (*Borago officinialis*) hA, 1½-2'. Large 1,2
hairy leaves. Sow direct early spring, loose loamy
soil, moisture, sun. Good companion plant for
strawberries, tomatoes. Young leaves for greens,
salad; improves flavor of cabbage. Tea exhilarating,
relief of rheumatism; good bee forage.

M,D **BROOM, SCOTCH;** (*Cytisus scoparius*) hP, 3'. 1,3
Shrub, yellow pea-like flowers in June. Used for
jaundice, kidney and bladder complaints. Yellow
dye.

M,I **BUCKWHEAT, WILD, St. Catherines Lace;** 1,3
(*Eriogonum Fasciculatum*) [Eriogonum] hP, 2'.
Shrub, dry, sandy location, full sun. Long blooming
season, white to pink flowers in clusters or heads.
Good bee plant, source of rutin. Tea for headache,
eyewash, high blood pressure, bladder ailments.

M,C **BURDOCK;** (*Arctium Lappa*) hB, 2-6'. Flowers 1,4
purple; root and seed used, valuable in salves, wash
for burns, boils, scurvy eczema and all skin diseases;
rheumatic and hysterical disorders; eases pain,
relieves udder congestion in dairy animals. Young
leaf stalks edible.

C,M **BURNET, SALAD;** (*Poterium Sanguisorba*) 1,3
[Sanguisorba minor] hP, 2'. Leaves for flavoring, in
salads. Moderately dry poor soil, sun. Green all
winter in most areas; tonic, astringent to staunch
bleeding, diarrhea, dysentery.

C,M **BURNET SAXIFRAGE;** [Pimpinella saxifrage] P, 1,3
3'. Leaves used as a salad herb, cucumber-like taste.
Root medicinal, aromatic, carminative. White
flowers in globular heads about June. Will self-sow.

I,C **CALENDULA, Pot Marigold;** (*Calendula of-* 3,4,1
ficinalis) hA, 2'. Cool weather flowers, sow in fall
for early spring blooms, golden yellow to orange.

Used as food coloring, will discourage nematodes in soil.

D   **CALLIOPSIS;** (*Coreopsis tinctora*) [Calliopsis tinctora] hA, 1'. Red to yellow flowers, very pretty, will self-sow. Dye plant.   1,2

M   **CAMPHOR TREE;** (*Cinnamomum Camphora*) Aromatic shrub or tree. Grow first in pot, then set out in permanent location. Wood distilled to produce camphore. Calming for nerves, sprains, diarrhea.   2,3

C   **CAPER BUSH;** (*Capparis Spinosa*) [Capparis] A, tP. Flower buds sold as capers. Warm, sunny location.   1,3

C,M   **CARAWAY;** (*Carum Carvi*) B. Sow seeds where plants are to remain for two seasons. Light, dry soil, full sun. Young shoots and leaves to flavor salads. Seeds produced second year, used to flavor bread, cake and cheese.   3

C   **CARDOON;** (*Cynara cardunculuc*) A. Related to globe artichoke, used for its blanched stalks, thick main roots. Use like celery, endive.   1

C   **CAROB, St. John's Bread;** (*Ceratonia Siliqua*) [Ceratonia] Small tree, produces edible fruit, substitute for chocolate. Tender, but will take a few degrees of frost. Can be grown as a tub or patio plant in colder areas. Soak seed three to four days before sowing.   1,3

M   **CASCARA SAGRADA;** (*Rhamnus Purshiana*) Deciduous tree to 20 feet. Bark used as mild laxative, acting principally on large intestines. Suitable for elderly and delicate persons; tonic, promotes digestion. Also used in veterinary medicine. Seeds planted in fall in prepared beds produce seedlings next spring.   3

M,I   **CASTOR BEAN;** (*Ricinus communis*) [Ricinus] A, tP, 5-10'. Easily grown shrub or tree, start indoors in pots, transplant after frost, good rich soil. Perennial   1,2 in south. Repels flies, gophers, moles. Fast growing. SEEDS MAY BE POISONOUS, but pods are easily clipped off before seeds form.

C,M,I   **CATNIP;** (*Nepeta Cataria*) hP, 3'. Dry, sandy soil,   1,2,3
sun. Whorls of pinkish flowers July to Sept. Used to reduce fever, abdominal gas. Attractive and exciting to cats. Catnip tea sprinkled over plants will discourage ants, insects.

CATNIP, PERSIAN; (*Nepeta Mussinii*) hP. Smaller, daintier leaves, trailing habit, can be used in hanging pots, lavender-blue flowers.

CATNIP, LEMON; (*N. Cataria cv. Citriodora*) hP. 3'. Whole plant has a pleasant lemony fragrance.

C,M   **CAYENNE, Bird Pepper;** (*Capsicum annum*   1,2
longum)1. Sun, rich soil, warm temp. Used as spice, medicinally to equalize blood pressure.

M,D   **CELADINE, GREATER;** (*Chelidonium majus*) hP,   1,2
2'. Yellowish-green foliage and yellow flowers. Broken stems yield an acrid orange juice. Plant yields natural dye. Used as a soothing eye lotion — one part brew to one part raw milk; for warts and corns, ringworm, use raw juice. Diuretic, for jaundice.

C   **CELERIAC, Rooted or German Celery;** (*Apium*   1,2
graveolens var. rapaceum) A. Rich garden soil, moisture, full sun. Root is edible part, for flavoring meats, soup, stews, served cold in salads. Sliced roots can be dried for off season use.

M,H   **CHAMOMILE, GERMAN;** (*Matricaria recutita*)   1,2
[Martricaria chamomilla] 1, 15". Dry, light, sandy soil, full sun. Self sows easily. White ray florets. Helpful to other plants in garden, good compost activator. The healing "Blue Oil" is warming, soothing, softening. Do not cover seed.

M,H   **CHAMOMILE, ROMAN;** (*Chamaemelum nobile*)   1,2
[Anthemis nobilis] P. Low growing, good for groundcover, spreads from root. Used for teas, and

by some persons as rinse for blond hair.

M,H   **CHAMOMILE, HUNGARIAN**; (*Chamaemelum nobile*) P. A very low, dense mat, smaller flowers. All three varieties — flowers only used for teas, medicinal purposes.

D   **CHAMOMILE, DYER'S, Golden Marguerite**;   1,2
(*Anthemis tinctoria*) P, 2-3'. Yellow, daisy-like flowers.

C,M   **CHERVIL**; (*Anthriscus cerefolium*) A, 18-24''. Rich   1,2
soil partial shade. Used in salad, fish sauce, with cooked vegetables. Smells like anise. Dried plant used externally for bruises, local tumors.

C,M   **CHICORY**; (*Chichorium intybus*) B, 2-4'. Rich,   1,2
deep soil, full sun. Used as greens; roots roasted as coffee substitute. Blanched heads as witloof or French endive. Good for stomach upsets.

C   **CHIVES**; (*Allium Schoenprasum*) P, 6-8''. Rich   1
soil, full sun, chopped leaves used for seasoning, fish, potatoes, eggs, sauces, salad.

M,H,C   **CLARY SAGE**; (*Salvia sclarea*) B, 3'. Blue-white   1,3
flowers, large wooly foliage, very fragrant. Oil used in perfumes dried leaves for sachets, to flavor wines and ale; used medicinally for eyes, weak backs.

M,H,D   **CLEAVERS, Goosegrass**; (*Galium Boreale*) [Galium   1,3
aparine] P, to 3'. Bristly. Seeds one of best coffee substitues — dry, then roast lightly and brew. Whole plant, except root, used medicinally as diuretic, tonic, alternative laxative. Tea for quiet, restful sleep, wash for sunburn and freckles. Ointment for scalds and burns. Roots make a red dye.

M   **CLIMBING FUMITORY**: (*Adlumia fungosa*), hA.   1,2
Climbing plant with pretty fern-like leaves, large clusters of pinkish or purplish tube-shaped flowers June and July. Prefers partially shaded location, well-drained, moist. Blood purifier, skin disorders, milk crust on scalp of infants, tonic.

M,C   **CLOVER, RED;** (*Trifolium pratense*). Valued for its   1,2
alkaline property, flowers used, either eaten raw in
salads or for tea. Good for blood cleansing, soothing
to nerves, promotes sleep and restores fertility. One
of the few herbs known to exert a beneficial in-
fluence on all types of cancers.

C,M   **COLTSFOOT;** (*Tussilago farfara*) P. Prefers poor,   3,4
moist soils along stream banks. Flowering stem
appears about February with yellowish flower head,
much later large, hoof-shaped leaves develop. Both
parts used medicinally. Demulcent, expectorant,
tonic, cough remedy, herbal tobacco. Fresh foliage
used as a vegetable.

M,C   **COLTSFOOT, SWEET;** (*Petasites*) [P. var.   1,3
speciosa] hP, 1-2'. Very large leaves, deeply cleft, 7-
9'' long. Light purple flowers appear before leaves,
bloom in March, and are very sweet scented. Leaves
and young stems cooked as vegetable. Stems and
leaves, dried and burned — ashes used as salt substitute.

M,C   **COMFREY;** (*Symphytum asperum*) hP, 3'. Leaves   1,3
and root used for teas, poultice for healing wounds,
inflammations. Nutrative pot herb. Easily grown in
most garden soils. Best started from roots — see
plant list section of catalog.

D   **COREOPSIS;** (*Coreopsis lanceolata*) P, 18''-3'.   1,2
Double, golden yellow flowers 2'' across, bloom
summer through fall.

C,M   **CORIANDER:** (*Coriandrum sativum*) A, 12-18''.   1,2
Dry, light, medium rich soil, full sun. Leaves in
salad, chinese dishes, seeds in pastry, cookies,
pickling spice, fruits. Soothing to stomach, add to
laxative herbs to prevent gripping. Plant as companion to carrots.

C   **CORN SALAD;** (*Valerianella Locusta*) [V. olitoria]   1,2
A. Pot herb or salad, ready within two months, good
for winter greens.

M   **CORYDALIS, Fumitory;** (*Corydalis lutea*) P, 1-2'.   1
Attractive fernlike foliage, flowers resembling

bleeding hearts bloom in April. Light, well drained
soil, partial shade. Gentle tonic. Slow to germinate,
freeze seed two weeks before sowing.

C,H,M **COSTMARY, Alecost, Bible Leaf;** (*Chrysanthemum*   1,3
balsamita var. tanacetoides) hP, 2-3'. Leaves used
for sachets, nice lemony fragrance. For potpourri; in
salads for aroma and taste. Astringent, antiseptic.

C **COW PARSNIP;** (*Heracleum giganteum*)   1,3
[Heracleum] 6-10'. Parsley family, for bold effect.
Large white umbels of flowers one foot or more
across. Young shoots for pot herb, salad. Seeds sown
in fall germinate in spring. Ash from burnt foliage
used as salt substitute.

M **COWSLIP;** (*Primula officinalis*) hP, 8". Fragrant   2,3
yellow flowers, sow seed in May or June in fine soil,
do not cover seed. Prefers cool location, summer
shade. Set in beds in October for spring blooming.
Flowers sedative, antispasmodic; roots for muscular
rheumatism.

C **CRESS, GARDEN, Pepper Grass;** (*Lepidium*   1,2
sativum) A. Quickly grown salad green. Cut often.
Adds agreeable pungent flavor to salads.

C,M **CUMIN;** (*Cuminum Cuminum*) A. Easily raised,   1
finely cut leaves, seeds ingredient in curry powder,
for flavoring pickles, soup.

M **DATURA STRAMONIUM;** A, to 5'. Erect white or   1,2
violet flowers, prickly fruit. A valuable medicinal
herb, but narcotic and POISONOUS.

C,M,H **DILL;** (*Anethum graveolens*) A, 3-4'. Sow seeds   2,3
where plants are to remain. Medium rich, sandy,
well-drained soil, sun. Leaves used in cottage cheese,
sauces, potato salad. Seeds for pickles, vinegar,
pastry, perfume, soap. Tea for colic, gas, to stop
hiccoughs; seeds chewed to sweeten breath.

M,C **DITTANY OF CRETE, Hop Marjoram;** (*Origanum*
Dictamnus) P. Same uses as sweet marjoram or
oregano. Good for tea. Pretty, grey downy foliage,

hop-like pink flowers. Nice in rockery or hanging pots.

C,M   **DITTANY, WHITE, Gas Plant;** (*Dictamus albus*)   3,1
P, 2½'. Rich soil, sun or part shade. Plant in fall, seeds germinate in spring or freeze seed two weeks before sowing. Lovely rock plant. Medicinal tea from blossoms. Lemon scented, substitute for China tea. Was used as protection against contagious disease. Foliage emits an ethereal inflammable oil.

DITTANY, PINK; (*Dictamnus albus, var. rosea*) A pink flowering variety of the above.

M   **DUSTY MILLER;** (*Senecio Cineraria*) [Cineraria   1,2
maritima] A, 10''. Sterilized juice of plant used for capsular and lenticular cataract of eye. White foliage, small yellow flowers. Very pretty edging plant. Do not cover seed after sowing.

M,D   **DYER'S GREENWOOD, Dyer's Broom;** (*Genista*   1,3
tinctoria) hP, 3'. Shrub, yellow pea-like flowers, used to dye wool yellow.

M   **ECHINACEA,   Coneflower;   (*Echinacea*   2,3
angustifolia) [E. purpurea] P, 3'. Fresh root used medicinally. Increases bodily resistance to infection; for boils, erysipelas, septicaemia, cancer, syphilis and other impurities of the blood. Lovely flowers in a rich deep reddish purple, full sun.

C,M   **ELDER, Blueberry elder, Sweet elder;** (*Sambucus*   1,3
I,D   *nigra*) hP, 8-10'. Shrub or tree. Flowers in large, creamy-white umbels, dark blue-black berries used for pies, jelly. Has many medicinal uses. Repels insects. Grows easily, prefers partial shade, moisture. Soak seed overnight before planting.

M,C   **ELECAMPANE;** (*Inula helenium*) hP, 4'. Large,   1,3
D,I   yellow daisy flowers, good border plant. Average soil, sun. Violet-scented root used for candy, medicinal, stomach tonic. Steam baths for stiffness and rheumatism. Dried and powdered as insecticide. Root for blue dye.

M   **ENGLISH DAISY**; (*Bellis perennis*) P. Low   1,3
growing, with pretty red or pink many-petalled
flowers. Celebrated as a wound herb, leaves are
used, also for stomach and intestinal problems,
headache. Dislikes hot, dry locations.

M   **ENGLISH HAWTHORNE**; (*Crataegus monogyna*)   3
hP tree to 30'. Heart remedy. Soak seed, plant in
fall. White flowers in spring, followed by red berries.

C,M   **FENNEL, FLORENCE**; (*Foeniculum vulgare duice*)   1,2
hA, B. Rich, well drained soil. Bulb-like base
blanched and cooked as vegetable, or raw like celery,
but sweeter, more aromatic. Seeds-condiment; leaves
for salad, seafood, add to juices. Medicinally as
compress or eye bath for inflammation, watering of
eyes; to increase flow of mother's milk; in drinks for
slimming.

C,M   **FENNEL, RED, OR BRONZE**; (*Foeniculum*   1,2
vulgare) P, 4-5'. Foliage reddish-bronze, very ornamental. Seeds have sweet licorice flavor, used for
flavoring, salads, pickles, facial packs, slimming.
Soothing to stomach, use with herbal laxatives to
prevent gripping.

M,I   **FENUGREEK**; (*Trigonella foenum-graecum*) hA,   1,2
2'. Clover-like white flowers. Seeds used medicinally
as poultice for wounds, abscesses. Tea for throat
gargle, inflamed stomach, intestines. Oil of seed
imitation maple flavoring. Seed powdered and mixed
with water repels insects.

M,I   **FEVERFEW**; (*Chrysanthemum parthenium*) hP, 2'.   1,2
Blooms June to Sept. Small, profuse flowers, yellow
heads with white petals. Readily grown from seed.
Tea used for fevers, tonic and vermifuge. Leaves
steeped in alcohol, dabbed on skin to repel insects.
Do not cover seed after sowing.

M,I   **FEVERFEW, GOLDEN**; (*C. parthenium, var
Aureum*) hP, 2'. Foliage lighter, greenish-yellow,
flowers single, but more profuse than above — same
uses.

M   **FIGWORT**; (*Scrophularia*) hP, 2'. Serrated leaves, reddish-purple flowers. Used for all cutaneous eruptions, abscesses, wounds. Fresh leaves made into ointment.   1,3

M,H   **FLAX, BLUE**; (*Linum perenne*) hP, 2½. Deep blue flowers early May. Seeds laxative. Fresh herb for rheumatic pain, colds, coughs and dropsy.   1,2

M,H   **FLAX, RED**; (*Linum grandiflorum, cv rubrum*) [Linum rubrum] A,1½. Sow seeds where they are to stand, full sun after frost is past. Scarlet flowers, very pretty.   2

M,I   **FLEABANE, ORANGE**; (*Erigeron Aurantiacus*) hP, 3". Warm, sandy soil, sun. Orange, daisy-like bloom. Pungent, tonic, diuretic, astringent, insect repelling. Very attractive.   1,2

I   **FLEABANE, PURPLE**; (*Erigeron specious*) hP, 2'. Numerous aster-like flowers.   2,3

M   **FOXGLOVE**; (*Digitalis purpurea*) B, 3-5'. Ornamental bell-shaped flowers; second years' growth of leaves used medicinally, yields digitalin, a heart stimulant. Grows easily, likes some shade.   1,3

C,M,I   **GARLIC CHIVES**; (*Allium tuberosum*) hP, 18". White, star-like flowers in clumps. Used for seasoning, for aphid control around roses and other plants.   1,2,3

I,M   **GERMANDER**; (*Teucrium chamaedrys*) hP, 6". Spreading habit rosy flowers. Stimulant, aromatic; nice clipped as low hedge for border.   1,3

M   **GINSENG**; (*Panax quinquefolius*).

M   **GOAT'S RUE**; (*Galega officinalis*) P, 3'. Bright green, smooth leaflets, lilac or white flowers, likes deep soil and moisture. Autumn planting is best. Diaphoretic, acts to lower blood sugar in diabetes; refreshing foot bath for tired feet; increases lactation in cows.   1,3

C,M   **GOBO, Edible Burdock;** (*Arctium lappa sativa*) B.   2,3
First year roots an excellent vegetable, second year
flower stalks vegetable or salad. One of the best
blood purifiers.

D   **GOLDEN DAISY;** (*Anthemis tinctora*) A, 18".   2
Yellow flowers, full sun, used for yellow dye.

M,D   **GOLDENROD;** (*Solidago Odora*) hP, 2-3'. Large   1,3
racemes of golden yellow flowers. Fragrant,
aromatic, diaphoretic, stimulant, beverage tea; dye
plant.

I   **GOPHER SPURGE;** (*Euphorbia lathyris*) B, 2-4'.   1,2
Striking plants, easy, full sun. Will drive gophers and
moles from garden. Being grown experimentally as
source of crude oil.

M,D,I   **GORSE;** (*Ulex europaeus*) [Ulex] P to 6'. Dense   3
evergreen shrub, semi hardy, fragrant yellow
flowers, grows in poor, sandy soil. Decoction of
flowers for kidney gravel or stones, obstructions of
liver and spleen. Dye plant.

M   **GUM PLANT;** (*Grindelia robusta*) hP, 2'. Used for   1,3
asthma, bronchial conditions, whooping cough and
kidney disease. Large yellow flowers, sun, poor soil.

D   **GYPSYWORT;** (*Lycopus europaeus*) hP, 30". Dye   1,2
plant, produces permanent black on silk or wool.

M   **HEARTSEASE, Wild Pansy;** (*Viola tricolor*) A,4".   1,3
Flowers purple, yellow and white, very pretty massed
as ground cover for bulbs; self sows easily. Blooms
from early spring through summer. For skin
diseases, inflammation of lungs, chest; asthma and
epilepsy. Strengthens heart.

M   **HEDGE NETTLE;** (*Stachys ciliata*) hP, 3-4". Bright   1,3
red-purple flowers June-July. Shade or partial sun,
moist areas. Plant somewhat coarse looking, but
suitable for back of borders or wild garden. Has

reputation as healing for cuts and bruises.

| H | **HENBANE**; (*Hyoscyamus Niger*) hA or B, 2½'. Greenish yellow funnel-shaped flowers, veined purple. Leaves and flowering tops antispasmodic, hypnotic, mildly diuretic. Similar in action to Belladonna and Stramonium, though milder in its effects. Externally relieves pain of gout and neuralgia. | 1,2 |

| M | **HEMP AGRIMONY**; (*Eupatorium cannabinum*) P, 2-5'. Pleasant aromatic fragrance, flowers light purple or nearly white. Blood purifier, for influenza and jaundice. | 1,3 |

| M,H | **HOPS**; (*Humulus lupulus*) hP, Twiner to 18'. This is not polypoid, as all polypoid hops are sterile. Soak seed till it sinks, then sow and keep cold 35-40°F. for several weeks, bring indoors to warm place to sprout. | 3,4 |

| M | **HOREHOUND**; (*Marrubium vulgare*) hP, 1-3'. Thrives in poor light soil. Used for candles, tea for colds, cough. | 1,3 |

| M | **HOREHOUND, BLACK**; (*Ballota nigra*) hP, 4-5'. Antispasmodic vermifuge, strong unpleasant scent. | 1,2 |

| M | **HOUND'S TONGUE**; (*Cynoglossum grande*) P, 12''. Serrate, rough bristly leaves, reddish purple flowers (borage family) used internally and externally to relieve piles, also soothing to digestive organs, coughs, catarrh. | 1,3 |

| M,I,C | **HYSSOP**; (*Hyssopus officinalis*) hP, 2-3'. Full sun, limey soil. Good bee plant. Used in salad, aids digestion of fat meat, flavoring for sausage, fruit cocktail and fruit pies. Compress for wounds, prevents black and blue marks, tea for coughs, colds. Pretty deep blue flowers. | 1,2 |

HYSSOP, PINK; (*Hyssopus off. cv Rosea*) same as above with rosy pink flowers, blooms later than blue.

M   **HEDGE HYSSOP;** [Gratiola], hP, 1-2'. Cathartic,   1,2
emetic for scrofula, liver, spleen, jaundice. Likes wet
places.

D   **INDIGO;** (*Indigofera suffruiticosa*) tP, to 6'. West   1
Indian shrub, used to produce blue dye.

D   **INDIGO;** (*Indigofera tinctoria*) tP, to 6' (as above).

M,H,D **INDIGO, WILD;** (*Baptisia australus*) P, 3-5'. Deep-   1
cut, light green foliage, indigo-blue profuse flowers,
resembling lupine, good cut flower, easily grown.
Sun or part shade. Roots and leaves antiseptic,
stimulant, purgative. For tumors, ulcers. Dye plant.
Soak seed before sowing.

D   **INDIGO, WILD;** (*Baptisia tinctoria*) hP, 18''.
Smaller, shrub-like plant with very small, dainty
foliage, small yellow flowers.

      INDIGOBUSH; (*Amorpha fruticosa*) P, large shrub   1,2
to 20'. Dark purple to pale blue flowers in 6'' long
clustered spike. Easy from seed, fast growing. Sunny
location, dry soil.

M   **JACOB'S LADDER, Greek Valerian;** (*Polemonium*   1,3
caeruleum) hP, 1-2'. Deep, rich well-drained soil. No
lime. Feather shaped leaves, bright blue flowers.
Coughs, colds, fevers, nervous complaints,
headache, epilepsy.

      JERUSALEM SAGE; (*Phlomis fruticosa*) hP, 4'.   1,3
Evergreen shrub. Large, downy leaves, yellow
flowers in wooly heads in June. Very decorative.

M   **JOE-PYE-WEED, Queen of the Meadow;**   3
(*Eupatorium purpureum*) hP, 4'. For fever, influenza, skin diseases, diarrhea, tonic. Likes ample
moisture.

C,H   **JO-JO-BA;** (*Simondsia chinesis*) tP. Evergreen   1,2,3
shrub, thick leathery leaves, brown acorn-like fruit
contains nutritious oil, eaten raw, roasted or parched
for coffee substitute. Oil used for hair oil, waxes,
varnish, candles. Not hardy below 15°F.

M **JUPITER'S BEARD, Red Valerian;** *(Centranthus* 1,2
ruber) hP, 3'. Fragrant, coral-red flowers in dense
terminal clusters, June and July. Flowers diuretic,
tonic; roots for diarrhea, sedative without side effects. Showy.

M **KINNIKINICK;** *(Arctostaphylos Uva-Ursi)* hP. 1,3
Prostrate creeping shrub, small, shiny evergreen
leaves, red berries later summer. Diuretic, astringent,
tonic. Used in diabetes, kidney ailments, smoked as
herbal tobacco.

M,C **LADIES MANTLE;** *(Alchemilla vulgaris)* P, 12". 2,3
Very pretty, with tiny flower clusters, stems and
leaves all green, clothed in soft hairs. Rootstock
astringent, edible. Whole herb — astringent, styptic,
wound herb, for excessive menstruation.

C,M **LAMB'S QUARTERS;** *(Chenopodium album)* A. 1,2
Nutritious tasty green, used like spinach.

C,M **LAVENDER;** *(Lavendula)* P, 1-3'. Lavender-blue 2,3
H,I flowers, compact habit, very fragrant. Loose, sandy
soil, good drainage, sun, add lime to soil. Transplant lavenders every four to five years. Stimulant,
tonic, for headache, fainting. Perfumes, sachets, for
moths and mildew odors.
   Varieties:
**LAVENDER VERA, English lavender, True
lavender;** *(L. Angustifolia)* [L. Vera]. Hardy,
fragrant, an old favorite.

SPIKE LAVENDER; *(L. Angustifolia)* [L. spicata]
3-4'. Broader leaf, longer flowering spikes.

LAVENDER MUNSTEAD; *(L. Angustifolia, cv.
Munstead)* Improved strain of Vera, dwarf.

PINK LAVENDER; *(L. Angustifolia cv. Rosea)* [L.
Spicata Rosea] A pale pink flowering variety.

LAVENDER STOECHES, French Lavender; *(L.
Stoeches)* Compact, dark purple, squarish flowers,
used in perfumes.

FRENCH DENTATE LAVENDER; (*L. Dentata*) Dentate grey-green foliage, blooms almost continuously, not hardy.

SPANISH DENTATE LAVENDER; (*L. dentata*) Dentate greenish foliage, not hardy, continuous blooming.

FERN LEAF LAVENDER; (*L. Pinnata*) Ferny grey foliage, very pretty, blooms continuously.

C,M   **LEMON BALM;** (*Melissa officinalis*) hP, 3'.   1,3
Medium dry, sandy soil, sun or part shade. Bruised leaves give strong lemon scent. Use with fruit, iced teas, salads, dressings, mushrooms. Will keep bees from stinging if rubbed on skin. Tea has a calming effect, promotes rest and sleep.

M   **LEOPARD'S BANE;** (*Doronicum cordtatum*) P,   1,3
12". Daisy-like yellow flowers early spring. Easily grown, likes partial shade, rich soil. Used to heal wounds externally.

C,M   **LIME BALM;** (*Melissa var.*) Same as Lemon Balm, except with a distinct LIME fragrance.

M,C   **LICORICE ROOT;** (*Glycyrrhiza glabra*) hP, 3'.   2,3
Pale blue flowers, rich, moist soil. Coughs, chest complaints, to flavor other medicines. Seeds erratic in germination, seedlings subject to damp-off.

M   **LOBELIA, Indian Tobacco;** (*Lobelia inflata*) A, 18-   1,2
24". Yellowish-green flowers, does best with some shade from hot afternoon sun. Used externally as lotion for congested chest; skin ailments, bruises and sprains. For epilepsy, cramps, obstructions, all spasmodic ailments; emetic.

M   **LOBELIA, BLUE;** (*Lobelia siphilitica*) hP, 18".   1
Moist soils, half shade, blue flower. Expectorant, stimulant, emetic.

C,H   **LOVAGE;** (*Levisticum officinalis*) [Lingusticum   1,2,3
scoticum] hP, 18". Rich, moist soil, well composted. Aromatic seeds used in cakes, pot herb, for

seasoning, teas. Bath herb to improve circulation and as deodorant. Keep seeds in dark to germinate.

I   **LYCHNIS, Campion, Catchfly;** hP. Members of the   1,2
Pink family with glue-like substance on the stem which is said to catch flies, insects.
    Varieties:
L. ALPINA; 3-4". Rose pink flowers in dense terminal clusters, good rock garden plant.

JERUSALEM CROSS; (*L. Chalcedonia*) 3'. Dense heads of bright scarlet flowers.

GERMAN CATCHFLY; (*L. Viscaria*) [Viscaria vulgaris] 1'. Rose flowers.

ROSE CAMPION; (*L. Coronaria*) 4'. Bright fuchsia-red flowers, downy-grey foliage.

L. VISCARIA SPLENDENS; 3'. Large heads of rose-pink flowers.

SWEET WILLIAM CATCHFLY; (*Silne armeria*) 16". Pink flowers.

M,D   **MADDER;** (*Rubia tinctorum*) P. Leaves in whorls   1,3
around stem which has a way of reclining as it elongates; can be supported by trellis, or allowed to sprawl and take root. Dye plant for reds.

M,C   **BLUE MALLOW, Common mallow;** (*Malva*   1,2,3
Sylvestris) P, 3-4'. Flowers bright mauve-purple with dark veins. Leaves and flowers used for coughs, colds, poultices. Foliage cooked for wholesome vegetable, seeds edible.

M,C   **MUSK MALLOW;** (*Malva moschata*) P, 2'. Rose colored flowers, three times the size of common mallow. Leaves, root and flowers used, similar properties to common mallow.

C,M   **MANZANITA;** (*Arctostaphylos species*) hP. Shrub,   3
grey-green foliage, edible berries, medicinal leaves for poison oak. Slow to germinate, can be treated with sulfuric acid, or stratify.

I,D   **MARIGOLDS;** (*Tagetes*) A. Marigolds may be started early indoors. Set out after danger of frost is gone. Full sun. Plant near tomatoes to protect from horned tomato worms, also repellent to other insects.
    Varieties:

CHRYSANTHEMUM, FLOWERED; 2-3'. From golden lemon to deep orange, large flowers.

DWARF; 10''. Double, yellow, orange, maroon. Plant a pretty border around vegetables to deter pests.

MEXICAN; (*Tagetes pumila*) 7''. Single golden yellow flower, orange eye; makes a compact, rounded mound, profusely blooming.

TAGETES MINUTA; 6-10'. Flowers, pale yellow late in season. This plant has root secretions that act as selective weedkiller and soil pest destroyers. Effective against ground elder, convolvulus, destroys eelworms. Cut for compost in Nov. Soil conditioner for clay soils. Plant 8'' apart, each way.

D   **MARGUERITE, GOLDEN;** (*Anthemis tinctoria*)   1,3
hP, 2'. Yellow or orange flowers, dye plant. Two varieties: *Kelwayi* — Lemon yellow flowers to 3'; *St. Johannis* — 1-2'. Bright golden orange.

C,M,H   **MARJORAM, SWEET;** (*Origanum majorana*)   1,2
[Marjorana hortensis] tP, 8-10''. Usually grown as annual.Light, medium rich soil, full sun. Used for soups, sauces, egg, chicken, meat dishes. Medicinal tea for indigestion, colic, headache, tonic.

C,M,H   **MARJORAM, POT;** (*Origanum heracleoticum*)   1,3
[Origanum onites] hP, 1-2'. Hardier than Sweet Marjoram, same uses, more pungent flavour.

M,C   **MARSHMALLOW;** (*Althaea officinalis*) hP, 4'.   1,2
Flowers pale rose with purple stamens, easily grown in any good garden soil, sun or some partial shade, moisture. Root used for food. Demulcent and

emollient; for poultice, wasp and bee sting, sore throat, colds, urinary organs, dysentery.

M **MEADOW RUE;** (*Thalictrum aquilegifolium*) hP,   1,3
1-2'. Light, rich loamy soil, shade. Easily grown decorative border plant, fern-like foliage, white, purple, orange flowers. Contains "thalicarpine," an alkaloid that has an inhibitory effect on intramuscular tumors.

M **MEADOW SAFFRON;** (*Colchicum autumnale*) P.   3
Used in medicine for gout and arthritis. Root and seed anti-rheumatic, cathartic and emetic. Sow direct in summer for seedlings next spring. Flowers purple or white, like crocus.

M,D **MEADOWSWEET;** (*Filipendula ulmaria*) [Spiraea   1,2,3
ulmaria] hP, 2'. Contains acetylsalicylic acid (the synthetic is called aspirin) in natural form, can be used wherever aspirin is used without its side effects: rheumatism, arthritis, kidney and bladder complaints. Fragrant white flowers in June.

C,M **MERCURY, GOOD KING HENRY;**   1,2,3
(*Chenopodium Bonus Henricus*) hP, 1'. Rich, well-drained soil. Leaves and shoots for pot herb, like spinach. Young thick shoots boiled like asparagus. Poultice of leaves for healing, roots given sheep for cough, to fatten poultry.

M **MORMON TEA, EPHEDRA;** (*Ephedra viridis*) P,   2,3
3'. Dry, gritty soil. Green stemmed shrub, contains ephedrine. Tea, used for cough, cold, headaches, fevers.

M,D **MOTHERWORT;** (Leonorus cardica) hP, 5'.   1,3
White tomentose flowers. Excellent bee plant. Antispasmodic, tonic, nervine, emmenagogue, for female weakness, heart problems. Green dye.

C,M *THE MINTS:* prefer rich moist location. Flavoring   1,3
I,H for foods, beverages, tea for indigestion. Repel insects, flies and rodents; hP, 1-3'.

Varieties:

PEPPERMINT; (*Mentha peperita*)

VARIEGATED PEPPERMINT; (*M. peperita var.*)
Attractive green and white variegated foliage.

SPEARMINT; (*M. Spicata*)

CURLED MINT; (*M. spicata cv. crispata*) [Mentha crispata]

APPLE MINT; (*M. suaveolens*) [M. rotundifolia]

PINEAPPLE MINT; (*M. Suaveolens varigata* [M. rotundifolia varigata] A nice fruity flavor with pretty variegated foliage.

LEMON MINT; (*M. peperita var. citrata*) [M. citrata]

EAU DE COLOGNE MINT; (*M. peperita var. citrata eau de cologne*) [M. citrata var. eau de cologne]

WATER MINT; (*M. aquatica*)

EGYPTIAN MINT; (*M. Niliaca*)

LICORICE MINT; (*Agastache anethiodora*)

KOREAN MINT; (*Agastache rugosa*) An important medicinal plant in Taiwan.

M,I   **MONARDA, BEE BALM;** (*Monarda didyma*) hP, 2-3'. Scarlet flowers long blooming season; grow in borders in veg. garden to dispel insects. Tea for digestive upsets. Good bee plant.   1,2

M,I   **MOUNTAIN MONARDA;** (*Monardella odoratissma*) hP, 1'. Small bushy plant, very aromatic. Pale rose-purple flowers in May, June. Very pretty. Used by Indians for stomach upsets.   1,3

M,I,C   **MUGWORT;** (*Artemisia vulgaris*) hP, 2-4'. Dry, chalky soil full sun or part shade. Leaves for cooking with pork or goose to neutralize fat. Flavoring for   1,3 beer. Tea for digestion, rheumatism, foot baths, repells insects, pests.

M,D   **MULLEIN;** (*Verbascum phoeniceum*) hP, 4'. Purple, red flowers. Fine for borders; moist, well-drained soil, full sun.   1,3

M   **MULLEIN;** (*V. phoenicium, native species*) hP, 3-5'. Large, pale pink flowers, light green foliage, smooth above, down beneath.   1,3

M,D   **MULLEIN;** (*V. Thapsus*) hB, 8-10'. Woolly leaves, white or more often yellow flowers. One of the best known herbal cures for deafness of middle ear due to catarrh, for pectoral complaints, bleeding of lungs and bowels. Demulcent, emollient, slightly sedative. For cough, asthma, toothache.   1,3

M,C   **MUSTARD, BLACK;** (*Brassica nigra*) hA, 6'. Young leaves for salad, table mustard, easily grown cool weather plant. Cut before seeds form so it will not spread. Turn under for green manure, to cleanse pastures.   1,3

C,M   **NASTURTIUM, large;** (*Tropaeolum majus*) A. Showy red, orange, yellow flowers bloom continuously through summer on large climbing plants; seeds and leaves pickled (Indian cress) also used for salad. Antiseptic for blood and digestive organs, nervous depression, tiredness, poor sight. Treatment of all worms, poultice for abscesses, boils, styes.   1,2

H   **NEPETA GRANDIFLORA;** hP, 3'. Flowers blue, foliage has pleasant, delicate fragrance.   1,2

M,I   **NETTLES;** (*Urtica dioica*) hP, 3-6'. Has course
C , D   stinging hairs. No sting when dried or cooked. Grows in fertile ground, likes rich soil. Use as cooked greens, in soups, dried in salad. Diuretic, increases haemoglobin, rich in minerals and vitamins. Hair rinse. One of best compost activators; keeps flies away. Tonic, blood cleanser for kidneys, lymphatic ailments, dropsy, anemia, rheumatism, sciatica, obesity, infertility. One of the most chlorophyll-rich plants. Nettle juice can be made in a   1

juicer. Juice provides antidote for its own sting. Fibre similar to hemp or flax, but smoother and stronger. Green and yellow dyes.

C,M,D **OREGON GRAPE;** (*Mahonia aquifolium*) [m.   3
aquilofolium] hP, to 6'. Evergreen shrub, fruit for jams; medicinal root. Yellow flowers, blue-black berries in fall. Seed can be sown in prepared beds, sandy soil in the fall.

C,M,H **OREGANO;** (*Origanum vulgare*) hP, 1-2'. Well-   1,3
drained, sunny location. Used in Italian, Spanish, Mexican dishes, in tomato sauces, pizza. Tea for indigestion, headache, nervous complaints. Reddish-purple flowers.

C,M,H **OREGANO, WHITE;** (*Origanum vulgare cv. viride*)   1,2,3
hP, 1-2'. Foliage somewhat smaller than above, green bracts, flowers white. Better flavor.

I,H,D **OSAGE-ORANGE;** (*Maclura pomifera*) hP.   1,3
Deciduous, medium-sized tree or shrub, bright green leaves, large greenish-yellow, orange-like fruits, which are said to drive out cockroaches when hung in room. Not edible. Durable wood used for fenceposts, bow making. Dye plant. More than one necessary for pollination. Soak seed before sowing. Easily grown.

C   **PAPRIKA;** (*Capsicum annum grossum*) A. Red   2,3
fruits for seasoning mild, culture as for bell peppers.

C,M   **PARSLEY, PLAIN OR ITALIAN;** (*Petrosalinum*   1,3
crispum var. neapolitanum) [P. Hortense] B, 2'. Long germination — to eight weeks. Richer flavor than curly type. Prefers rich, well worked soil, partial shade. Leaves to flavor stew, soup, salad, potatoes. Tea for rheumatism, flatulence, kidney, bladder and prostate disorders. Rich in vitamins and minerals.

C,M   **PARSLEY, HAMBURG ROOTED;** (*P. crispum*
var. tuberosum) [P. sativum] B. Root used medicinally as diuretic. Leaves culinary.

M,C   **PASSION FLOWER VINE**; (*Passilfora incarnata*)   1,3
tP. Outdoors in south, pots or greenhouse in colder
areas. A lovely vine with beautiful flowers, white
with purple center. Fruit edible, used for juices and
jellies. Antispasmodic, sedative, narcotic. Soothing
for headache, neuralgia, promotes sleep; soothes
hysteria, spasms and convulsions. Start seed indoors,
germination takes 50-60 days. Pot in leaf mold and
fibrous loam. Roots near surface, do not hoe or
spade around plants.

C   **PATIENCE, SPINACH DOCK**; (*Rumex patientia*)   1,2
hP. Savory winter vegetable.

D,M   **PEARLY   EVERLASTING**;   (*Anaphalis*   1,3
margaritacea) hP, 2-3'. White wooly foliage, whitish
flowers. Dry for winter bouquets. Astringent, expectorant, for ulceration of mouth, aphrodisiac,
aromatic, antiseptic. Dye plant. Very pretty with
long-lasting, abundant flowers.

M   **PELLITORY-OF-THE-WALL**;   (*Parietaria   of-*   1,2
ficinalis) hP, 1-2'. Medicinal, according to Grieve
"the most effacious remedy for bladder stone, gravel
. . . all urinary complaints."

C,M,I   **PENNYROYAL**; (*Mentha pulegium*) hP, 14". Likes   1,3
clay, moist soil, part shade. Clean, minty scent. Used
in vinegars, jellies, beverages. Tea for headache,
nausea, constipation, colds, hang-overs. Repels
mosquitos, flies, fleas. Creeps to make a mat-like
ground cover.

C,M   **PEPPER**; (*Piper nigrum*) tP. Used as seasoning,   1,2
stimulating to mucus membranes, aids digestion.
BLACK PEPPER is the unripe fruit, the milder
WHITE PEPPER comes from the same vine when
allowed to ripen. Adaptable as a houseplant, partial
shade, constant moisture.

M   **PERIWINKLE**; (*Catharanthus roseus*) [Vinca   1,2
Rosea] A, 1-2'. White, pink flower.

M   **PERIWINKLE, MADAGASCAR**; (*Catharanthus*   1,3
roseus) [Vinca rosea] 1-2'. Tropical shrub, leaves

source of alkaloid for treatment of leukemia, some cancers, diabetes.

PINEAPPLE WEED, WILD CHAMOMILE; 1,3
(*Matricaria matricariodes*) A, 6''. Foliage and flowers very similar to other chamomiles, flowers have a delicate pineapple fragrance. Used for tea.

C,M **PLANTAIN;** (*Plantago major*) P. Low growing, 1,3
wound herb, poultices, bites and stings. For dysentery, diarrhea, ulcers, fevers. Leaves can be eaten in salad.

M,C,D **PLEURISY ROOT;** (*Asclepias tuberosa*) hP, 2-3'. 2,3
Start seed May to August in flats, erratic germination to 30 days. Keep moist, half shade. Plant outdoors in full sun, no lime. Splendid cut flowers, attractive to butterflies, yellow-orange flowers in September. Tubers, flowers, seed pods and shoots have been used for food. Used for all chest complaints, diarrhea, rheumatism, eczema. Yellow dye.

M,D,C **POKE;** (*Phytolacca americana*) hP, shrub to 6'. 1,3
Ornamental. Young shoots eaten like asparagus. Used for skin diseases, felons, rheumatism, hemorrhoids, also reported of value in breast cancer. Berries used for dye, tanning. Berries and mature plant considered non-edible, probably poisonous.

M,C **POPPY;** (*Papaver somniferum*) A, 2-4'. Double 1,3
fringed, carnation flowers. Seeds, flowers used for poultice, cough syrup. Seeds culinary. Sow in late fall or early spring for early spring germination. Resents transplanting.

M **POPPY, CALIFORNIA;** (*Eschscholzia californica*) 1,3
A or P, 2'. Juice reported mildly narcotic, used by Indians for toothache.

POPPY, ORIENTAL; (*Papaver orientale*) P, 3'. 1,2
Huge flowers in mixed colors from palest pinks, apricot, orange, deep scarlet. Sow in spring, set out in late summer or fall to bloom following spring. A spectacular display. Long lived, better left undisturbed after planting.

M   **POTENTILLA, CINQUEFOIL;** (*Potentilla Palustris*) [P. propinqua] hP, low growing, strawberry-like foliage, red flowers. Full sun. Nerve sedative, general astringent. For wounds, sore mouth or gums, ulcerated throat, sinus infections, epilepsy.   1,3

M   **POTENTILLA, TORMENTIL;** (*P. erecta*) [P. tomentilla] hP, 1''. Yellow flowers on slender stems (rare medicinal variety from West Asia). Nerve sedative, gargle — uses as above.   1

C,M   **PURSELANE;** (*Portulaca oleracea*) A. Trailer, used for green salads. Medicinally for inflammations, ulcers, hemorrhoids.   1,2

I,H   **PYRETHRUM, RED;** (*Chrysanthemum coccineum*) [C. roseum] hP, 1-2'. Attractive, finely cut foliage, daisy-like red and pink flowers which are dried and used as non-toxic insect powders. Use on pets for fleas, dust plants, or spray with soap as a spreader. Commercially used in Persian powder.   1,3

I,H   **PYRETHRUM, WHITE;** (*Chrysanthemum cinararifolium*) hP, 1-2'. Profuse white daisy-like flowers, yellow centers. Same uses as above. Used commercially in Dalmation powder, and grown commercially in U.S. for pyrethrum insect sprays. Non-toxic.   1,3

M,D   **QUEEN ANN'S LACE, Wild Carrot;** (*Daucus carota*) hP, 1-3'. Whole plant, root and seed medicinal. For dropsy, kidney, bladder and gout. Yellow dye.   1,3

M   **RAUVOLFIA SERPENTINA;** Shrub or tree, pantropical, roots source of tranquilizing drug.

C,M,D   **RHUBARB, Pie Plant;** (*Rheum rhabarbarum*) [Rhaponticum] hP, 2'. Stems for pie or sauce. Raw stems as bowel tonic and mild laxative. Roots for strong purge. In small doses root will ease diarrhea, dysentery, headache, jaundice and all liver troubles. Stems, stalks for dye.   1,2

C   **RED ORACH;** (*Atriplex hortensis cv. rubra*) A, 4'.   1,3

Pot herb, use like spinach. Domesticated relative of
Lamb's Quarters. Will self sow.

M   **RINGWORM SENNA**; (*Cassia Alata*) P, shrub to   1,3
8'. Flowers yellow in spike-like racemeṣ. Sun, sandy
loam, greenhouse plant in north. Notch seed coat to
hasten germination.

M   **ROCK ROSE, Sun Rose**; (*Helianthemum num-*   1,3
malariuna) H, 1'. Small shrub, dry, limestone soil,
full sun, good for border or rockery. Long flowering
period in shades of pink, rose. Aromatic, astringent,
gargle for sore throat, venereal diseases, cancer.

M   **ROCK ROSE**; (*Cistus ladanifer*) [C. villosus] hP, 4'.   1,3
Evergreen shrub with whitish, rose-like flowers.

C   **ROCKET, Rucola**; (*Eruca sativa*) B. Fast growing   1,2
green for salad.

M,C,H   **ROSEMARY**; (*Rosmarinus officinalis*) P, shrub to   2
6'. Light blue flowers, pine-like foliage, fragrant.
Sow seeds in April, slow germinating. Sun, light dry,
limy soil. Needs protection from heavy frost. Tonic,
astringent diaphoretic, stimulant, nervine for
stomach, headache, wash or rinse for hair to con-
dition and prevent dandruff. Popular seasoning
herb.

C,M   **RUE**; (*Ruta graveolens*) hP, 2'. Poor, heavy soil,   1,3
I,D   well-drained, full sun. Leaves used sparingly for
flavoring. Rutin from rue, to treat fragile capillaries.
A bitter, aromatic stimulant for gas pains, colic. Repels insects in garden. Attractive blue-green foliage,
yellow flowers. Root for red dye.

C,M   **RUE, CORSICAN**; (*Ruta corsicana*) Same as above,
I,D   but prettier, fuller foliage and flowers.

     RUE, BLUE MOUND; (*R. graveolens 'Blue
Mound'*) hP, 4'. A larger plant, giant leaved variety
of rue.

M   **RUPTUREWORT**; (*Herniaria glabra*) hP. Low   1,2,3
creeping plant, groundcover, rockery. Diuretic for

kidney and bladder, aids elimination of sodium and urea without increasing flow of urine.

C,M,
I,H
SAGE, GARDEN; (*Salvia officinalis*) hP, 1½'.　1,2,3
Sunny, dry location, good, well-drained garden soil.
Seasoning for dressing, sausage, cheese. Used as a
hair rinse, therapeutic baths, gargle, fevers. Repels
many insect pests.

SAGE, MEADOW, Meadow Clary; (*Salvia* 　1,2
pratensis) hP, 1-3½'. Large, crinkly foliage, flowers
in violet-blue spikes.

H,C,
M,I
SAGE, WHITE; (*S. apiana*) P, 2-3'. Sunny, dry 　1,2,3
location. Silvery leaf forms whorls on stem, very
decorative. Has pleasant flavor for culinary use.
Bees make excellent honey from this one. Needs
protection from heavy frost.

C,M
H,D
SAFFLOWER; (*Carthamus tinctorius*) A, 1-3'. 　1,2
Profus orange flowers in thistle-like heads. Seeds
produce oil for culinary purposes. Flowers laxative,
diaphoretic, similar uses to Saffron: for infants
diseases, measles, fevers, skin eruptions. Also for
dyes, rouge making. Oil for leather dressing,
illumination and culinary uses.

M,D
ST. JOHN'S WORT; (*Hypericum perforatum*) hP, 　1,3
1-2'. Ornamental yellow flowering heads.
Astringent, for bruises, bites, burns, rheumatism,
arthritis, nerves, jaundice, earache. Dye plant.

C
SALAL; (*Gaultheria shallon*) hP, to 6'. Large, 　3
leathery evergreen foliage, urn-shaped white or pink
flowers in spring and summer, followed by blue-
black fruits. Used by early settlers for making syrup,
pies, or dried and used as a meal. Foliage is the
'Lemonleaf' of florists. Partial shade, moist peaty
soil.

M,H,I
SANTOLINA; Lavender Cotton, hP, 2'. Border 　1,2,3
plant, moth repelling, used in sachets.
Emmenagogue, remedy for worms in children,
infused in vinegar for rheumatism rub. Yellow
button-like flowers.

Two varieties:

GREY SANTOLINA; (*Santolina chamaecyparissus*)
Silvery grey foliage.

GREEN SANTOLINA; (*S. Virens*) [S. Viride]
Feathery green foliage.

M   **SARSAPARILLA;** (*Aralia hispida*) P, 3'. Woody   1,2
shrub. Bark used for kidney, urinary diseases.

C,M,D   **SASSAFRAS;** (*Sassafras albidum*) P. Deciduous   3
tree, all parts spicy, aromatic. Bark yields oil of
sassafras. Root bark used medicinally, leaves for
condiment. Wood and bark for yellow dye.
Ornamental.

C,M   **SAVORY, SUMMER;** (*Satureja hortensis*) A, 12".   1,2
Does best in rich, moist soil. For seasoning, pleasant
spicy fragrance, used with vegetables, beans, pork,
stuffing. Companion plant for beans.

C,M   **SAVORY, WINTER;** (*Satureja montana*) hP, 6-   1,3
12". Poor, light well-drained soil, full sun. Good bee
plant. Use with stuffing, pork sausage; cook with
peas, beans, with turnips and cabbage to reduce
strong odor. Used medicinally for digestive
problems, colds; crushed leaves for bee sting. Can be
kept clipped into a neat border hedge.

C   **SAVORY, MINT;** (*Calamintha grandiflora*)   1,2
[Satureja grandiflora] hP, 12-18". A hardy savory
with a minty flavor, deep pink flowers.

M,C,I   **SEA HOLLY;** (*Eryngium maritimum*) hP, 2'. Silver   3
grey, with steel blue foliage, spiked stiff; flowers
blue, honey-scented. Good cut or dried. Light, rich
soil, sun. Plant in fall to germinate in spring, needs
cold to germinate, or freeze seven days before
planting seed. Roots, young shoots edible. Rich in
minerals. Nerve-tonic properties for liver, chest
ailments, gland deficiency, constipation; tonic,
aromatic, stimulant.

M   **SELF HEAL, ALL HEAL;** (*Prunella vulgaris*) hP,   1,2,3
8-12". Low growing leaves 1" long, purplish blue

flowers in dense terminal spike, pretty. Used for sore throat, internal bleeding, leucorrhea; wound herb. Well-drained, sunny location.

C,M   **SESAME;** (*Sesamum indicum*) A, 2'. Plant early in   1,2
spring. Seeds used to flavor bread, rolls, oil; added to green salad.

C   **SHALLOTS, FRENCH, Red Shallots;** (*Allium*   1,2
ascalonicum) A multiplier type onion, with a special, more delicate flavor. Can be pulled while green and used like scallions, or harvested when mature. They store well, can be left in ground all winter as they are hardy. A must for French cooking.

M   **SHEPARD'S PURSE;** (*Capsella bursa-pastoris*) A,   1,2
12". Whole plant infused to stop bleeding, internal or external.

I   **SHOO-FLY PLANT, Peruvian Ground Cherry;**   2
(*Nicandra physalodes*) A, 1-3'. Full sun or partial shade. Moderate rich garden soil. Delicate blue flowers. It is said that insects which feed on its sap are destroyed. Repels flies when in bloom. Repels white fly in greenhouse. Not toxic.

M   **SKULLCAP;** (*Scutellaria lateriflora*) hP, 12". For   1,3
all nervous disorders, epilepsy, convulsions, delirium tremens, wakefulness, headache, neuralgia. Also for sterility — internally and as a douche.

I,H,M   **SOAPWORT;** (*Saponaria officinalis*) P, 1½-2½'.   1,3
Root and leaves lather when agitated in water. Substitute for soap in shampoo. Remedy for scrofula and skin diseases.

H,M   **SOAPWORT, TRAILING;** (*Saponaria ocymoides*   1,2
cv. Rosea) hP, 8". Evergreen groundcover, nice for rockery, completely covered with profuse pink flowers spring and early summer. Very pretty.

C,M   **SOLOMON'S SEAL, FALSE; False Spikenard;**   1,3
(*Smilacina racemosa var. amplexicaulis*) hP, 1-3'. Moist, shady areas. A single stem, with large alternate leaves 8" long and a terminal cluster of

creamy-white, fragrant flowers about 6'' long in April, May, followed by a reddish berry. The plant inclines at an angle of about 30 degrees. Young shoots used as potherb. Berries edible, purgative in large quantities.

C,M **SORRELL, FRENCH;** (*Rumex scutatus*) hP, 18''.   1,3
Rich soil, part shade, adequate moisture. Sour taste, used as seasoning in salad, soup, greens. Rich in Vitamin C, considered to have blood cleansing properties.

M,C **SPICEBUSH, Wild Allspice, Benzoin;** (*Lindera*   3
benzoin) hP. Small tree, all parts have spicy, agreeable flavor, use for tea, flavoring; medicinal. Soak seed before sowing.

M   **SQUILL, SEA ONION, PREGNANT ONION;**   2
(*Urginea maritima*) Tender bulb. Sow seed in spring in pots of sandy soil. Large bulb half out of soil. Small bulblets emerge from its sides. Shiny dark green, strap-like leaves up to 3' long, flowering stem 1-3' high with long spike of green and white flowers. Nice house plant. Used in medicine as "Vinegar of Squill," etc. Bulb poisonous if ingested in large quantity.

C   **SWEET CICELY;** (*Myrrhis odorata*) hP, 2½'. Rich   3
soil, humus, full sun or partial shade. Finely cut, fragrant foliage, white flowers in large umbels. Used for flavoring, garnishes, as a vegetable. Add when cooking fruit to reduce acidity and use less sugar. Sow seed in fall, germinates after winter freeze. Good in rainy area, likes moisture.

M,I,C **TANSY;** (*Tanacetum vulgare*) hP, 3'. Likes dry,   1,3
sunny location, heavy soil. Creeping rootstock — can be invasive. Leaves used in pudding, cottage cheese, sprinkled over meats to preserve. Ant and insect repelling. Used for embalming in ancient days. Yellow, button-like flowering heads.

M,I,C **TANSY, CURLED;** (*T. vulgare, var. crispum*) hP,   1,3
3'. Finer feathery foliage, prettier. Same uses as above.

C   **TARRAGON, RUSSIAN;** *(Artemisia dracunculus)*   1,3
[A. dracunaloides] hP, 2'. Good drainage, full sun,
sandy loam. Use with fish, chicken, herb vinegars.
Flavor inferior to French Tarragon, but if left in
same spot will improve greatly and after 3 years
almost equal to French.

M,D,H **TEASEL;** *(Dipsacus fullonum)* [d. sylvestris] B, to   1,3
6'. Lavender flowers in dense heads. Seed heads
sharp, spine-like, used to raise nap on woolen cloth
in textile industry. Good to fluff angora sweaters.
Dried heads have many decorative uses. Good bee
plant, easily grown. Teasel water used for eye
ailments, styes, sores on fingers, wrinkles. Infusion
of root to stomach is liver remedy. Yields yellow
dye.

THRIFT, SEA PINK; *(Armeria maritima)* hP, 1'.
White to deep rose flowers, full sun, dry, light soil,
good drainage. Makes a pin-cushion-like mold, nice
for rockery.

M   **TOOTHACHE PLANT;** *(Spilanthes acmella)* 6''.   1,2
Yellow conical flower heads. Contains spilanthos, a
larvicidal with anesthetic properties on mucosa.

C,M,I   *THYME:* hP. Full sun, light, sandy, well-drained   1,2,3
soil. Important culinary herb. Used in linaments,
toothpaste, soaps, antiseptic. Tea for colds,
headache.

    Upright varieties:
GARDEN THYME, ENGLISH THYME; *(Thymus
vulgare)* 8-12''. Broad leaf, easily grown for culinary
use.

FRENCH, SUMMER THYME; *(T. vulgare var.)* 8-
12''. Grey foliage, pale lavender flowers, a culinary
favorite.

LEMON THYME; *(T. vulgare citriodora)* 8-12''.
Lemon scented foliage, good with fish, teas.

GOLDEN LEMON THYME; *(T. vulgare
citriodorus 'aureus')* Lemon scented, bright golden
edged foliage in spring.

SILVER THYME; (*T. vulgare 'argenteus'*) 8''. Dainty, silver-edged foliage.

DWARF THYME; (*T. vulgare var.*) 4-6''. Lower growing, green foliage.

Thyme, Creeping varieties:
WILD THYME; (*T. serpyllum*) Creeping, sweet-scented foliage.

MOTHER-OF-THYME; (*T. praecox*) Creeping, sweet-scented foliage, purple flowers.

RED CREEPING THYME; (*T. nummularius*) Covered with rosy-mauve flowers in spring.

WHITE MOSS THYME; (*T. praecox albus*) Dainty green foliage, white flowers. This one can take a little more shade than others.

M   **VALERIAN, GARDEN HELIOTROPE;** (*Valerina officinalis*) hP, 3-6'. Easily grown. Fragrant pale pinkish or white flowers. Full sun, or partial shade. Dried rhizome yields the drug Valerin, used as nervine, allays pain.   1,3

M   **VERONICA SPEEDWELL;** (*Veronica latifolia*) [V. teucrium] hP, 1'. Open sunny location or light shade. Good rock garden plant. Gentian blue flowers. Tonic, diuretic.   3

M   **VERVAIN;** (*Verbena officinalis*) hP, 2-3'. Easily grown, sun. Astringent, antispasmodic, diaphoretic. For fevers, poultices, neuralgia, rheumatism.   1,2,3

M   **VIOLET, SWEET;** (*Viola odorata*) hP, 6''. Bloom February to April, rich soil, partial shade. Sow seeds in flats in fall, leave out all winter in snow etc. Many reputed medicinal uses; laxative, for poultices, consumption, throat, headache.   3

Varieties:
BLUE; Deep blue-purple flowers.
PINK; Bright, rosy-pink flowers.
MIXED COLORS

C,M   **WATER CRESS**; (*Nasturtium officinale*) Grows   1,2
alongside and in flowing streams, springs.
Antispetic, tonic, nervous ailments, for internal
tumors and cysts including uterine cysts. Eat raw,
chopped in salads or cheese. Watercress soup: cook
with milk, garlic, butter and cayenne.

M,H   **WAX MYRTLE, CANDLEBERRY**; (*Myrica*   1,3
pensylvanica) H, 8'. Shrub bears clusters of waxy
aromatic berries in late July, used for making
Bayberry candles. Ornamental shrub.

D   **WELD**; (*Reseda luteola*) hP, 3-6'. Cool, moderately   1,2
rich soil, sow where they are to stand; resents
transplanting. Dye plant.

M   **WILD ALUM ROOT**; (*Heuchera micrantha*) hP,   1,3
6''. Beautiful foliage, green mottled and veined in
red, dark brown. Likes shade and moisture, good
house plant; astringent. Root eaten raw for diarrhea.

M   **WITCH HAZEL**; (*Hamamelis Virginiana*) hP.   2,3
Small tree or shrub. Yellow, flowers September and
October. Leaves, bark medicinal; astringent tonic,
sedative. Seeds germinate second year.

M   **WITHANIA SOMNIFERA**; Rare medicinal shrub   1,2
to 7', much smaller grown as pot plant. Partial
shade.

D   **WOAD**; (*Isatis tinctoria*) hB, 3-4'. Dye plant, yellow   1,3
flowers. Easily grown, full sun or light shade.

D   **WOODRUFF, DYER's**; (*Asperula tinctoria*) hP,   1,2
18''. Slender, dainty foliage, partial shade. Dye
plant.

C,M,   **WOODRUFF, SWEET**; (*Galium odoratum*)   3
H,D   [Asperula odorata] hP, 1'. Semi-shade, moist
location. Good ground cover under trees. Fragrant
tea, aids digestion, flavor for wines. Kept with linen
to preserve from insects. Whole plant fragrant,
especially when dried. Pretty foliage in whorls
around stem, white flowers in spring. Slow germinating. Sow in fall and expose to snow and frost.

C,M,I **WORMWOOD**; (*Artemisia absinthium*) hP, 3-4'.   1,3
Full sun, dry areas. Used in making Vermouth.
Tonic, aids digestion, strong bitter taste. Culpepper
states good for preventing drunkenness. Keeps
moths away, repels insects. Grey-white foliage.

M,I,D **WORMWOOD, AMERICAN, Sagebrush**; (*A.*   3
tridentata) hP, 3-4'. Dry, sandy soil, full sun. Grey-
green leaves, very bitter, terebinthine aroma, burning
leaves said to neutralize spraying by skunk. Good insect repellant.

M,I **WORMWOOD, SILKY**; (*A. frigida*) P, 8-12''. Soft,   3
silvery grey, silky foliage. Good rock garden plant.
Used medicinally for intestinal upsets, vomiting,
diarrhea, influenza. Repels insects, snails, slugs. Not
as bitter as the other wormwoods.

M,D *YARROW;* hP. Used for fevers, colds, to stop   1,2,3
bleeding, treatment for burns. Once established will
thrive through drought.

> Varieties:
> **WHITE YARROW**; (*Achillea millefolium*) hP, 3'.
> Double white flowers.
>
> **PINK YARROW**; (*A. millefolium, cv. Rosea*) hP, 3-
> 4'. Deep pink flowers.
>
> **YELLOW YARROW**; (*A. filipendulina*) hP, 4-5'.
> Large, flat, bright yellow flowering heads, very long
> lasting.
>
> **WOOLY YARROW**; (*A. tomentosa*) Makes a low,
> wooly mat with yellow flowers.
> Yarrows dry well for winter bouquets. Good for
> dyes, also help other plants in garden. They have
> attractive, finely cut foliage, long blooming season.

M **YERBA MATE**; (*Ilex Paraguariensis*) P. Evergreen   1,2
tree to 20 feet. Tub plant for greenhouse in cold
areas. Tea from leaves sustaining, tonic, diaphoretic,
stimulant.

M **YELLOW DOCK**; (*Rumex crispus*) hP, 2'. Root   1,2
laxative and mildly tonic for blood diseases, chronic
skin diseases, jaundice.

Everlasting flowers:

CHINESE LANTERN; (*Physalis alkekengi*) P. Orange, lantern-shaped pods.

CUPID'S DART; (*Catanache caerulea*) P, 2'. Blue, centaurea-like flowers.

CYNARA; (*C. cardunculuc*) P, 4-5'. Silvery foliage. Bronze-gold thistle-like seed heads for drying.

GLOBE AMARANTH; (*Gomphrena globosa*) 18''-2'. Ball shaped flower heads in bright pink, orange, reddish purple. Soak seed 3 days before sowing.

MONEY PLANT; (*Lunaria annua*) 18''. Silver-dollar like pods for drying.

SEA LAVENDER; (*Limonium vulgare*) Mixed colors. Soak seed two days before sowing.

STRAW FLOWER; (*Helichrysum bracteatum*) 3'. Brilliant mixture, large double flowers.

WINGED EVERLASTING; (*Ammobium alatum*) 3'. Solitary heads of yellow flowers surrounded by silvery white bracts. Easy, sow fall or spring. Perennial.

XERANTHEMUM annum; 2'. White, rose purple flowers, dainty and pretty.

—Compiled by the staff of
Casa Yerba, Days Creek, Oregon.

13

Directory

Associations, and where to buy herbs, seeds, starter plants, etc., in person or by mail order.

In addition to the outlets noted below, we suggest checking your telephone directory's yellow pages.

Herb sources

Aphrodisia
28 Carmine Street
New York, N.Y.   10014
(212) 989-6440

Herbs, spices, oils
Catalogue: 25 cents

Atlantis Rising Educational Center
7909 S.E. Stark Street
Portland, Ore.   97215

Catalogue — 130 pages; includes herbs, herb products, spices, oils, etc.

Back-of-the-Beyond Herbtique
c/o Shash Georgi
7233 Lower East Hill Road
Colden, N.Y.   14033
(716) 652-0427

Herbs, starter plants, seeds.

Borchelt Herb Gardens
474 Carriage Shop Road
East Falmouth, Mass.   02536
(617) 548-4571

Herbs, starter plants, seeds; free seed catalogue available — send stamped, self-addressed envelope.

W. Atlee Burpee Co.
300 Park Ave.
Warminster, Penn.   18974
(215) 674-4900

Mail-order seeds and plants. Free catalogue.

Calico Herbs
Newfame, Vermont   05345
(802) 365-4477

Herbal products, special seasonings (available also at wholesale), free catalogue.

Caprilands Herb Farm
Silver St.
North Coventry, Conn.   06238
(203) 742-7244

Herb plants, seeds, potpourris, catalogue — free; send self-addressed, stamped envelope.

Casa Yerba
Star Route 2, Box 21
Days Creek, Ore.   97429
(503) 825-3534

Organically grown starter plants, seeds.

Caswell-Massey Co., Ltd.
320 W. 13th St.
New York, N.Y.   10014
(212) 675-2210

Free catalogue.

Celestial Seasonings
1780 55th St.
Boulder, Col.   80301
(303) 449-3779

Wholesale seeds.

Comstock, Ferre & Co.
263 Main St.
Wethersfield, Conn.   06109

Annual & perennial starter plants, seeds; garden supplies, free
illustrated herb list.

J.A. Demonchaux Co.
827 North Kansas
Topeka, Kansas   66608

Dionysus' Barn
Box 31
Bodines, Penna.   17722

90 varieties of herb plants (retail & wholesale).
Brochure: 25 cents.

Enfleurage
Sue Anne Elmore
316 E. Main St.
Charlottesville, Va.   22902
(804) 977-0117

Herbs, teas, potpourris, etc.

Green Mountain Herbs Ltd.
4890 Pearl St.
Boulder, Col.   80302
(303) 444-3055

Wholesale.

The Grist Mill
6 Mill St.
Wolfeboro, N.H.   03894
(603) 569-2751

Herbs, spices in bulk.

Gurney Seed & Nursery Co.
Yankton, S.D.   57078

Harvest Health, Inc.
1946 Eastern Ave., S.E.
Grand Rapids, Mich. 49507
(616) 245-6268

Whole, cut & powdered herbs, 275 varieties; free catalogue.

Haussmann's Pharmacy
534-536 W. Girard Ave.
Philadelphia, Pa. 19123
(215) 627-2143

Unusual botanicals; herbal medicines, exotic oils & teas; Chinese & European herps. Free catalogue.

Helix Corp.
P.O. Box 1808
Boulder, Col. 80306
(303) 449-9432

Wholesale seeds.

The Herb Barn
Rte. 1, Box 256
Westfield, Ind. 46074

Herbal Home Products
Rescue, Calif. 95672

Medicinal herbal salves, botanical products (wholesale & retail). Free catalogue.

Herbally Yours, Inc.
P.O. Box 26
Changewater, N.J. 07831

Herbal delights, bulk herbs.
Catalogue: 50 cents.

Herbarium, Inc.
Route 2, Box 620
Kenosha, Wisc. 53140
(414) 857-2373

Botanical drugs and spices.

Herbs 'N Honey Nursery
c/o Mrs. Chester Fisher
Rte. 2, Box 205
Monmouth, Ore.   97361
(503) 623-4033
Catalogue: $1.

The Herb Society
c/o Mrs. George Dickey
14 Tupelo Rd.
Hilton Head Island, S.C.   29928

Hickory Hollow
Route 1, Box 52
Peterstown, W. Va.   24963
(304) 753-9817
Organically grown herbs, herbal products, seeds. Mail-order only. Not open to public. Catalogue: 25 cents, with stamped, self-addressed envelope.

Hilltop Herb Farm
Box 1734
Cleveland, Texas   77327
(713) 592-5859

Herbs, starter plants, seeds, unusual botanicals. Catalogue: 50 cents; send stamped self-addressed envelope. Retail & mail-order.

Indiana Botanic Gardens, Inc.
626 177th Street
Hammond, Ind.   46325
(219) 931-2480
Mail order and retail herbs.
Catalogue: 50 cents

Johnny's Selected Seeds
Organic Seed & Crop Research
Fuss Hill Road,
Albion, Maine   04910
(207) 437-9294
Seeds, small farm equipment, mail-order only; free catalogue.

Logee's Greenhouses
55 North St.
Danielson, Conn.   06239
(203) 774-8038

Rare herbs, exotics.
Color catalogue: $2.

Magus
P.O. Box 254
Cedar Grove, N.J.   07009

Herbs & spices, wild & organic (wholesale & retail).
Free catalogue.

Meadowbrook Herb Garden
Wyoming, R.I.   02898
(401) 539-7603

Seeds, plants, herbal products (wholesale).
Catalogue: 50 cents.

Merry Gardens
Camden, Maine   04843

Pot-grown herbs — culinary, decorative, medicinal, over 100 varieties.

Nature's Herb Co.
281 Ellis St.
San Francisco, Calif.   94102
(415) 474-2756

Herbal pharmacy, herb plants.
Catalogue: 25 cents.

Nature's Way
P.O. Box 2233
Provo, Utah   84601

Herbs, herb products & formulas.

Nichols Garden Nursery
1190 No. Pacific Highway
Albany, Ore.   97321
(503) 928-9280

Organically grown herbs & other plants, seeds, botanical products;
catalogue available.

Old Fashioned Herbs
Box 1000
Springville, Utah
(801) 377-4005

Herbs by mail-order only. Catalogue: 25 cents.

George W. Park Seed Co.
P.O. Box 31
Greenwood, S.C.   29647
(803) 374-3341

Flower & vegetable seeds; catalogue available.

Penn Herb Co., Ltd.
603 N. Second St.
Philadelphia, Pa.   19123
(215) 925-3336

Dried herbs, seeds, oils, other herbal products, plus Olbas products
imported from Switzerland. Free catalogue; phone order service.

Pickity Place
Nutting Hill Rd.
Mason, N.H.   03048

Herbs & country crafts.

Richters
Goodwood, Ontario
Canada   L0C 1A0

Over 300 varieties of herb seeds. Illustrated catalogue: 75 cents.

San Francisco Herb Co.
367 9th St.
San Francisco, Calif.   94103
(415) 861-7174

Mail-order and retail herbs, spices and oils. Free catalogue.

San Francisco Herb, Tea
   & Spice Trading Co.
2226 Union St.
San Francisco, Calif.   94123
(415) 346-6226

Herbs, spices, tea blends. Free catalogue.

Star-Crane Enterprises
N.Y. Paralab Distributors:
810 W. 183 St., No. 3E
New York, N.Y.   10033

All-natural formula pharmaceuticals, spagyrically prepared
Price list: 25 cents.

Sunnybrook Farms Nursery
Box 6
9448 Mayfield Road
Chesterland, Ohio   44026

Sunnypoint Gardens
Rte. No. 1
Egg Harbor, Wisc.   54209
Herb plants. Catalogue: 50 cents.

Taylor's Garden, Inc.
1535 Lone Oak Rd.
Vista, Calif.   92083
(714) 727-3485
Herb plants.
Catalogue: 50 cents.

W.J. Unwin, Ltd., Seedsmen
Histon
Cambridge, England
(U.S. address:
Squankum-Yellowbrook Road,
Box 9
Farmington, N.J.   07727)

Well-Sweep Herb Farm
317 Mt. Bethel Rd.
Port Murray, N.J.   07865
(201) 852-5390
Seeds, herb plants, herb products.
Price list: 35 cents.

Wide World of Herbs, Ltd.
P.O. Box 266
Rouses Point, N.Y.   12979
Botanicals, perfumes, seasoning, dyes, teas.

186 · A Book of Herbs

Wide World of Herbs, Ltd.
11 Saint Catherine St., East
Montreal, Quebec
Canada   H2X 1K3

Botanicals.

Thomas Woods
Box 64, Jefferson, N.H.   03583
(603) 586-7734

Over 80 varieties of herb plants; will mail. Catalogue available each
spring.

World Seed Service
Box 1058
Redwood City, Calif. 94064

Every kind of seed available (incl. rare herbs, medicinal & fragrance).
Illustrated catalogue: $1.

Yankee Peddler Herb Farm
Hwy 36N
Brenham, Texas   77833

Plants, seeds, botanicals, etc. Catalogues: herbs with uses: $2. Herbs
without uses: $1.

Associations

Bio-Dynamic Farming and Gardening Assoc., Inc., Box 253, Wyoming, R.I. 02898.

Herb Society of America, 300 Massachusetts Avenue, Boston, Mass. 02115

Organic Gardening Clubs of America, 33 East Minor Street, Emmaus, Pa. 18049.

About the author

EDITH FOSTER FARWELL spent her childhood in a small town outside Boston and later moved to Lake Forest, Ill., a northern suburb of Chicago, with her husband, Albert. Articles about her herb and vegetable gardens have appeared in *Famous Gardens of the World, Time,* the *Chicago Daily News* and *Chicago Tribune, Milwaukee Journal* and various specialty herb and gardening magazines. She was honored with many awards from American gardening organizations, and is shown here at work in her greenhouse during the winter of 1977, six months before her death. Her backyard herb garden was divided into culinary, medicinal, fragrant, historical and biblical sections. She grew her own table vegetables, fruits and grains, and for many years raised bees and chickens. To the west of her house was a duplicate of the Blair Kitchen Garden from Williamsburg, Va. A copy of her knot garden, thought by many to have been the best in the U.S., is now maintained at the Chicago Botanic Garden in Glencoe. Ill,

Notes

Notes

To order additional copies of this book, send $6.95 per copy to The White Pine Press, Box 402, Piermont, N.Y. 10968. Price includes postage and handling.